Powers of Attorney:
A Practical Guide

by John Thurston, LLB, Solicitor, Head of Department of Professional Legal Studies, School of Law, De Montfort University, Leicester

Second Edition

Tolley Publishing Company Limited

 A member of the Reed Elsevier plc group

ISBN 1 86012 434-8

First published 1991
Second edition 1997

Published by
Tolley Publishing Company Limited
Tolley House
2 Addiscombe Road
Croydon
Surrey
CR9 5AF
0181–686 9141

Typeset in Great Britain by
Action Typesetting Limited, Northgate Street, Gloucester

Printed and bound in Great Britain by
Hobbs the Printers, Southampton

Preface

Powers of attorney are granted frequently in various situations – the grantor may be going abroad for a prolonged period, or may be elderly. In the case of an elderly person, enduring powers, which are not revoked by the subsequent mental incapacity of the donor, are particularly useful. Powers of attorney are also found in commercial transactions, for example in mortgage and partnership agreements.

Powers of attorney may be granted to lay persons as well as to professionals, and I hope this book will serve its purpose and be of use not only to legal practitioners, but also to anyone who is asked to act as an attorney. Throughout this book I have referred to the donor or donee of the power as 'he' or 'him' – it is nothing more than a way of avoiding the slightly clumsy alternative of 'he/she' and 'him/her', and I apologise to female readers for any offence caused.

I am grateful to P D Lewis and R T Oerton for permission to use their material.

I acknowledge Crown copyright for the Acts of Parliament, statutory instruments, and orders and rules quoted or referred to in the text. Law Commission reports are reproduced with the permission of the Controller of Her Majesty's Stationery Office.

John Thurston

Contents

Table of Cases

Table of Statutes

Chapter 1

Introduction

1. What is a power of attorney?

A power of attorney is a deed by which a person confers power on another to act on behalf of the person granting the power. The person granting the power is called the donor, grantor, or principal, and the person on whom the power is conferred is called the donee, grantee, agent, or attorney. The power can be general or limited. If it is general, the donee, grantee, agent or attorney will be authorised to do anything which the donor, grantor, or principal could have lawfully done; if it is limited, the donee, grantee, agent, or attorney may have authority only to deal with one particular transaction, for example the sale of a house. The power may also be limited in time; it may expressly state that it is to remain in force for a specified period, or whilst the donor is abroad. As soon as the specified period expires, or the donor returns to the United Kingdom, the power will terminate.

For the sake of simplicity, in this book the person granting the power is usually called the donor, and the person to whom the power is granted is usually called the donee or attorney.

2. Typical uses

Powers of attorney are frequently granted when a person is about to go abroad for a prolonged period and may be difficult to contact. They are also granted in respect of short absences abroad, for example a holiday, if it is likely that action will have to be taken on behalf of the donor whilst he or she is away.

Elderly persons also appoint attorneys so that they do not have to deal with their business affairs. It is particularly appropriate for those persons who are confined to the house or are in a nursing home, who cannot get out to visit the bank or otherwise attend to their affairs.

In addition, a power of attorney may be incorporated into other transactions. In a mortgage, the mortgagor or borrower may give the mortgagee or lender a power of attorney to enable the mortgagee or lender to sell the property should the mortgagor or borrower default. A power of attorney is also often found in partnership agreements; the partners appoint each other their attorney so as to enable them to deal with partnership matters on behalf of each other. This power is particularly useful if a partner has left the partnership, perhaps because he or she has been expelled, and is not prepared to co-operate with the other partners. He or she may refuse to sign documents connected with the partnership; the continuing partners can sign the documents on his or her behalf if they have a power of attorney. Powers of attorney are also used in conveyancing transactions, for example where a house is purchased by a home relocation company.

3. Types of power of attorney

It is always open to the donor of a power to specify in detail the powers conferred on the attorney. These can merely authorise the attorney to enter into one transaction, or they can be so wide as to permit the attorney to do anything the donor or principal could have done. In the latter situation, before 1971 the power was usually very long (for example see *Midland Bank Ltd v Reckitt* [1933] AC 1).

Since the Powers of Attorney Act 1971, if a donor or principal wants to confer a general authority on the attorney, it has not been necessary to set out at great length the powers conferred on the attorney. Instead, use can be made of the general form of attorney set out in Schedule 1 to the Act, which gives the attorney authority to do any act which the donor could have lawfully done (s 10 Powers of Attorney Act 1971). The donee under this power will be able to operate bank or building society accounts on behalf of the donor, sell any house or other property belonging to the donor, and invest money on behalf of the donor. This power is reproduced on page 175, and it should be used if the donor or principal intends to grant a general power.

Frequently powers of attorney are granted by elderly donors, perhaps about to enter nursing homes, to adult children to enable the children to operate bank and building society accounts and deal with investments on behalf of their parents. The basic rule is that a power of attorney is revoked by the supervening mental incapacity of the donor, so that if a parent who has given a child a power of attorney becomes incapable of managing his or her affairs, the power of attorney terminates, and the child cannot continue to act under the power. In this situation the only way of dealing with the assets of the parent is to apply to the Court of Protection under the Mental Health Act 1983. Usually, the Court of Protection appoints a relative to be a receiver to manage the assets of the patient. The disadvantages of applications of this nature are the procedural requirements and the fees (for a further discussion, see page 9 of the Law Commission's report on *The Incapacitated Principal* (Law Com No 122 Cmnd 8977)).

The recommendations of the Commission were enacted in the Enduring Powers of Attorney Act 1985 ('EPAA 1985'). This authorises the creation of enduring powers of attorney which are not revoked by the subsequent mental incapacity of the donor.

4. Operation of enduring powers of attorney

This is dealt with in more detail in Chapter 7. In outline, the donor grants a general or limited power of attorney to the donee or attorney, using a prescribed form. The power is operated as an ordinary power, until the donee or attorney has reason to believe that the donor is or is becoming mentally incapable, whereupon the attorney must make application to the court for the registration of the power. Notice of application must be given to specified relatives, who can object to the registration on various grounds. Once the power is registered, the attorney continues to act, but the court has various supervisory powers. Thus an enduring power is not revoked by the supervening mental incapacity of the donor, although an ordinary power would be revoked in that situation. Enduring powers are accordingly very useful in the case of elderly donors as they enable the attorney to continue to act after the donor has become mentally incapable, provided they are registered.

5. Joint powers and joint and several powers

Frequently a donor will appoint one person to act as attorney. However, the donor does not have to appoint a sole attorney; he or she can appoint two or more persons to act as attorney.

If two or more persons are appointed, they will either have a joint power, or a joint and several power. The instrument creating the power should state which power is being created, because there is a difference between joint authority and joint and several authority.

If it is a *joint power*, all the attorneys must join in making any decision, so that one joint attorney cannot bind the others. If one joint attorney dies, the power terminates. On the other hand, if it is a *joint and several power*, all the attorneys do not have to join in making decisions, and one can bind the others. If one joint and several attorney dies, the others can continue to act.

Apart from the general importance of the distinction between joint powers and joint and several powers, the EPAA 1985 lays down different rules for these types of powers (see Chapter 7).

Typical uses

A donor of a power should always appoint as donee or attorney a person he or she can trust. However, there may be situations where it will cause offence if a person the donor distrusts is not appointed the attorney. For example, if there are several children living near a parent, it may cause offence if all of them are not appointed attorneys, even though the parent may distrust one of them. One way round this problem is for the donor to appoint joint attorneys so that they can act as a check on each other, as a joint attorney will not be able to deal with the property or money of the donor without the consent of the other attorney.

PD Lewis in *The Law Society's Gazette* (26 November 1986 at page 3568) poses the problem of a donor who has two children, neither of whom he wishes to alienate, but does not want to entrust sole management of his affairs to one. He suggests that the donor could grant two enduring powers – one appointing the donor's solicitor and one child, and the other appointing the solicitor again, and the other child.

Joint and several powers should be conferred when it is expected that one or more of the attorneys will sometimes be unable to act, for example because he or she goes abroad frequently, or because one or more of the attorneys is elderly, and may predecease the donor.

It is not possible to have a joint or joint and several appointment of three persons on the basis that only two of them could act [STEP February 1997 at page 6].

6. Is a power of attorney necessary?

If it is intended that the power should continue despite the supervening incapacity of the donor of the power, an enduring power must be granted. But if there is little possibility of the donor becoming mentally incapable, so that an enduring power of attorney is not appropriate, it may be that a power of attorney is not essential, and that the donee can do all that is required on behalf of the donor under a written or even an oral authority.

The grant of a power of attorney creates an agency relationship between the donor and the donee of the power. The basic rule is that no formalities are required for the appointment of the agent, and an oral appointment can be effective, although it is highly desirable that any appointment should be in writing in order to prevent disputes later, and to protect the donee against allegations that he or she has exceeded his or her authority. However, there are a few transactions where a power of attorney will be required. These are considered next.

(a) Transactions which require a deed

Certain transactions require a deed for their validity. Examples of transactions requiring a deed are:

(i) a conveyance of land. This must be made by deed under s 52(1) Law of Property Act 1925, and under s 205(1)(ii) 'conveyance' is defined as including a mortgage, charge, and a lease;

(ii) leases for more than three years (s 54(2) Law of Property Act 1925);

(iii) transfers or registered land (Land Registration Act 1925 and Land Registration Rules 1925).

The Law of Property (Miscellaneous Provisions) Act 1989 ('the 1989 Act'), the relevant provisions of which came into force on 31 July 1990, has altered the rules about deeds. Before the 1989 Act came into force, a deed had to be signed, sealed and delivered. The requirement of a signature has been given a liberal interpretation by the courts; it clearly includes a handwritten signature, but it has also been held to include a signature made with a rubber stamp (see *Goodman v J Eban Ltd* [1954] 1 QB 550, [1954] 1 All ER 763). The seal was at one time a very important requirement, and was an impression in molten wax. Today, the seal on a deed is usually a small red self-adhesive circle stuck on to the document; it can be purchased from any law stationers. 'Delivery' means showing an intention to be bound by the documents by acts or deeds, and originally this intention was shown by handing over the deed. Now frequently this intention will not be shown expressly, but will be inferred from the circumstances. For example, a donor who executes a power of attorney will usually be held to have intended to be bound by it immediately in the absence of any contrary intention. In addition, if a party to a deed wanted to confer authority on some other person to execute that deed, that authority had to be conferred by deed (*Berkeley v Hardy* (1826) 5 B & C 355, 108 ER 132).

The 1989 Act amended these rules. Section 1(3) provides that a deed must be signed by the person making it, or alternatively it can be signed by an agent at the direction and in the presence of the maker of the deed and in the presence of two witnesses who each attest the signature.

Section 1(1)(c) of the 1989 Act abolishes any rule of law which requires that a deed must be used to confer authority on another person to deliver an instrument as a deed; s 1(3)(b) provides that the deed must be delivered by the person making it or by a person authorised to do so on his behalf.

The effect of these provisions is that no authority by deed is necessary for an agent to sign a deed in the presence of the maker of the deed, or to deliver it whether or not the maker is present. However, a deed will normally have to be used to confer authority on the agent to sign a deed in the *absence* of the principal. A power of attorney is therefore essential if a donor is going abroad and wishes to confer authority on an agent to enter into a transaction which will require the execution of a deed whilst the donor is abroad.

(b) Transactions which do not require a deed

Under s 2(1) of the 1989 Act a contract for the sale or other disposition of an interest in land can only be made in writing, and under s 2(2) the contract must be signed by or on behalf of each party to the contract. However, there is no requirement of writing for the appointment of an agent to sign such a contract.

Section 1 of the Stock Transfer Act 1963 requires a transfer of shares to be executed by the transferor. Article 23 of Table A in the Companies (Tables A to F) Regulations 1985 (SI 1985 No 805) states that a transfer must be in any usual form or other form which the directors may approve, and must be executed by or on behalf of the transferor. There does not appear to be any requirement that a person executing a transfer on behalf of another should be authorised to do so by a power of attorney, but it is clearly desirable that this should be done in order to take advantage of the protection offered by ss 5 and 6 Powers of Attorney Act 1971. These sections are discussed in Chapter 12.

If the only assets of the prospective donor are money in a bank or building society account, the donee can be authorised in writing to operate the account, and most banks and building societies have a standard form of authority for this purpose. However, any such authority will be revoked by the subsequent mental incapacity of the donor, although most banks and building societies do not make enquiry about the mental state of the donor.

Thus an oral or written authority will often suffice, apart from the situations where the agent will be required to sign a deed in the absence of the principal. In addition, if it is intended that the authority should continue after the donor has become mentally incapable of managing his own affairs, an enduring power of attorney should be granted. It is also possible for a person to be appointed as an agent or appointee to collect social security benefits for another person.

7. The donee

The question of capacity is discussed in Chapter 9. In most cases, it will be appropriate to appoint from amongst the following:

(a) relatives;

(b) friends;

(c) solicitors;

(d) accountants.

The donor and the donee are often related. A person going abroad for a prolonged period may wish to appoint his spouse, or a parent, or a child as his attorney; an elderly donee may wish to appoint a child or a friend as attorney. In these situations the attorney will frequently not expect to be paid for the work he or she does in pursuance of the power. However, if there is no suitable relative or friend, a solicitor or accountant or other professional person may be appointed, and they will expect to be paid for the work they do as attorneys.

As will be seen later, there are few restrictions on who can be appointed attorney, but he or she should be a person whom the donor considers he or she can trust. There is always the risk that relatives or friends may use the power to benefit themselves rather than the donor of the power, and although they can be made to account for any misuse of money or property belonging to the donor, such right is of little use if the donee has no assets. If professional persons such as solicitors or accountants are appointed, is it unlikely that the power will be exercised otherwise than for the benefit of the donor. However, as mentioned earlier, professional persons will expect to be paid for their services, and if the assets of the donor are not very valuable, the expense may not be justified.

The Public Trustee will not accept an appointment as attorney (PD Lewis, *The Law Society's Gazette* (28 October 1987) at page 3083).

(The Public Trustee is an office created by the Public Trustee Act 1906. Fees are chargeable for the services provided by the Trustee, and he is not bound to act if appointed. However, he cannot refuse to act on the ground that the estate is too small.)

Summary

- A power of attorney may be desirable if a person is about to go abroad, or is elderly.
- A power of attorney can be general or limited in time or to a particular transaction.
- If a donor of a power of attorney is elderly, he or she should grant an enduring power, which will not be revoked by the supervening mental incapacity of the donor.
- More than one person can be appointed attorney.
- A power of attorney may not be necessary as an agent can be authorised orally or in writing to carry out many transactions.

Chapter 2

Powers of attorney and the elderly

1. When should an enduring power be granted?

This chapter is concerned with the practical aspects of when an enduring power should be granted. The question of when a donor has capacity to grant an enduring power is considered in more detail on pages 82–98. Whilst a donor should have a general understanding of what is being created, it is not necessary for the donor to have a complete understanding of what is happening. However, the donor must be able to understand the following:

(a) that the donee will be able to assume complete authority over the donor's affairs, if the power is unrestricted;

(b) that the donee will be able to do anything with the donor's property which the donor could have done, if the power is unrestricted;

(c) that the authority will continue if the donor should be or become mentally incapable;

(d) that if he should be or become mentally incapable, the power will be irrevocable without confirmation by the court.

(*Re K; Re F* [1988] 1 All ER 358 at page 363.)

It could be argued that as soon as a person attains 70, or even 60, he should grant an enduring power to any children. On the other hand, many people retain their faculties well into their seventies or eighties or nineties or even beyond, and they may not be very happy about entrusting the management of their affairs to their children. It is clearly an issue which may need tactful handling, although many people will readily grant such a power. They may also be reluctant to entrust all their affairs to a particular child; for a discussion of joint and several powers, please see pages 3–4.

Of course, the donor can continue to manage his own affairs despite the grant of an enduring power, and so it may be a good idea for a person to grant an enduring power on the understanding that it will not be exercised whilst the donor retains his faculties. Indeed, it is possible for the power to expressly state that it will not come into effect until some event occurs, for example the making of an application for registration of the power (see below). A joint power could be granted to two or more children; the effect of this would be that all the attorneys would have to agree to any action.

It is also clear that an enduring power can still be granted even though the donor is showing signs of mental incapacity. Thus it is possible to wait, but at the first signs of mental incapacity, an enduring power can be granted. Most people do not suddenly become incapable; it is usually a gradual process. On some days they will be fully capable; on other days they will not.

2. When should an enduring power be registered?

The duty to register an enduring power arises if the attorney has reason to believe that the donor is mentally incapable (s 4(1) EPAA 1985). As it could be difficult to decide precisely when a donor becomes mentally incapable, the section also provides that the duty arises when the attorney has reason to believe that the donor is becoming mentally incapable.

Many donors become incapable gradually, and it is best to register as soon as it becomes clear that the donor will not recover his mental capacity. It should be noted that once the duty to register has arisen, application for registration must be made as soon as practicable (s 4(3)).

3. Procedure for registration

In outline, the procedure is that the attorney must give notice to the donor and to various relatives of the donor. The attorney then has to apply to the Public Trustee for registration of the enduring power.

The relatives to whom notice must be given are specified in Sch 1 Pt I para 2(1) EPAA 1985. The first four specified are:

(a) the donor's spouse;

(b) the donor's children;

(c) the donor's parents;

(d) the donor's brothers and sisters, whether of the whole or half blood.

Notice does not have to be given to more than three persons, but if one person in a class is entitled to notice, then notice must usually be given to all the other members of the class (para 2(4)). This means that if the donor has a spouse and four children, it will be necessary to give notice to the spouse and all the children. It is more than likely that the attorney will be one of the children, but he does not have to give notice to himself (para 3(1)).

Notice must also be given to the donor, but the court has power to dispense with this requirement in certain circumstances (para 4(2)).

Form EP1 must be used to give notice to the relatives and the donor.

Rule 8 Court of Protection (Enduring Powers of Attorney) Rules 1994 (SI 1994 No 3047) requires that an application to register an enduring power of attorney shall be made in Form EP2. It must be lodged with the Public Trust Office not later than ten days after notice has been given to the donor and every relative entitled to receive notice.

4. Effect of registration of the power

The effect of registration of a power is to freeze the power. This means that the donor cannot revoke the power unless the revocation is confirmed by the court. In addition, the donor cannot extend or restrict the scope of the authority conferred by the instrument, and the attorney cannot disclaim the power without giving notice to the court.

5. Duties of the attorney

The duties of an attorney are varied, but they can be summed up very simply. An attorney must show the utmost good faith to the donor. This means that the attorney must keep accurate accounts, and if he wants to purchase property belonging to the donor, he must disclose all relevant facts. If the attorney is a solicitor, further duties may be imposed. Similar rules apply to other dealings with the property of the donor. Once the power has been registered, the court has power to consent to transactions of this nature.

Summary

- People in their sixties or older should consider granting an enduring power of attorney.
- An enduring power should be registered as soon as the donor becomes mentally incapable.
- Once a power has been registered, the donor cannot revoke, extend or restrict the operation of the power.

Chapter 3

Going abroad and powers of attorney

Although postal services are often quick, it may be considered desirable for anyone living or working abroad to grant a power of attorney. It may also be desirable that a person going abroad for an extended holiday should grant a power of attorney. The purpose of this chapter is to highlight some of the issues involved in connection with such powers.

1. Ordinary power or enduring power?

It seems that a donor living abroad can grant an enduring power, and thus it is clear that a donor resident in England and Wales, but contemplating a trip abroad, can grant an enduring power.

If the donor is young or middle aged, it would seem that an ordinary power is appropriate, although there is no reason why an enduring power should not be granted. On the other hand, if the donor is elderly, there is considerable merit in the grant of an enduring power in case the donor becomes mentally incapable; this would otherwise revoke the power.

2. Delegation by trustees

It may be that a person who is *a trustee and is* going abroad may wish to appoint a person to act on his behalf whilst he is abroad. This is possible under s 25 Trustee Act 1925 as amended by s 9 Powers of Attorney Act 1971. The delegation must be by power of attorney, and it must be for a period not exceeding twelve months. The delegation can be very wide; the attorney can be authorised to execute or exercise all or any of the trusts, powers and discretions vested in him as trustee either alone or jointly with any other person or persons. Note that under s 25(2) the person appointed attorney may include a trust corporation but not (unless a trust corporation) the only other co-trustee of the donor of the power.

Various formalities must be satisfied; these are discussed in more detail in Chapter 9.

Section 23(2) Trustee Act 1925 does permit delegation by trustees or personal representatives, but only in respect of property outside the United Kingdom.

Section 9 Trusts of Land and Appointment of Trustees Act 1996 provides that trustees can delegate any of their functions to any beneficiary or beneficiaries of full age and beneficially entitled to an interest in possession in land. The delegation can be for a set period, or indefinitely, but it cannot be done by an enduring power.

3. Grants of powers of attorney by co-owners

This situation is of course very common as the majority of houses are vested in the names of both spouses or cohabitants, who are trustees of the legal estate. If one co-owner is going abroad, he may want to delegate his powers, and often he will want to grant a power of attorney to his spouse or cohabitant. Section 10 Powers of Attorney Act 1971 forbids the use of the general power of appointment for this purpose, and under s 25 a trustee cannot delegate to another trustee. However, although the position is not without doubt, it seems that it may be possible to use an enduring power to appoint another co-owner as attorney. Section 3(3) EPAA 1985 authorises an attorney under a general or limited enduring power to execute or exercise without obtaining any consent, all or any of the trusts, powers or discretions vested in the donor as trustee. Also without the concurrence of any other person, the attorney may give a valid receipt for capital or other money paid.

4. Extent of the power

The power of attorney may authorise the attorney to do anything with regard to the property of the donor which the donor could have done. Alternatively, it may merely authorise the attorney to deal with a particular transaction, for example the sale of a house.

In the case of an elderly person, it is desirable that the power should be unlimited, and that an enduring power should be granted. If the donor becomes mentally incapable, the power will not then be revoked. On the other hand, if the donor is relatively young, it may be that only a limited power will be granted.

Section 25 gives a wide power of delegation, as does s 3 EPAA 1985. If a general enduring power is granted, it will authorise the attorney to deal not only with the trust property, but also with the personal property of the donor. Although in many cases there will be no harm in this, there may be cases where the power should be restricted.

The power of delegation contained in s 9 Trusts of Land and Appointment of Trustees Act 1996 is wide, but rather limited in its application.

Summary

- If a young donor is going abroad, an ordinary power is appropriate; otherwise use an enduring power.
- Trustees can delegate under various provisions.
- Co-owners can delegate to each other by means of an enduring power.

Chapter 4

Powers of attorney and professional persons

Solicitors and accountants are frequently appointed as attorneys. This chapter is aimed at highlighting some of the aspects which professional persons appointed as attorneys should consider.

1. Duties

Generally an attorney is not under a duty to act. However, if a client appoints a solicitor or an accountant as an attorney, it is probable that there is a contractual obligation on the attorney to act.

There is a general duty imposed on attorneys to keep accounts, and of course solicitors must comply with the Solicitors' Accounts Rules.

There is also a duty to take care and be skilful, and in the case of attorneys who are professionally qualified the duty is higher than that imposed on an unqualified person.

Is an attorney who is a solicitor entitled to benefit himself at the expense of the donor? The rule applying to all attorneys is that they must disclose all relevant facts. Is a higher duty imposed on attorneys who are solicitors and accountants? *The Guide to the Professional Conduct of Solicitors 1996* at page 278 states that a solicitor who is appointed an attorney must not use that power so as to confer a benefit on himself which 'he would not be prepared to allow to an independent person'. However, a solicitor should advise the donor of a power to take independent advice before exercising the power so as to enter into a transaction which benefits the attorney. If the attorney is acting under an enduring power which has been registered, application should be made to the court for directions as the court has power to authorise the donor to enter into transactions benefiting the donor of the power (s 8(2); see Chapter 7).

2. Rights

An attorney is entitled to be indemnified for all acts within the limits of the power; on the other hand, if he exceeds the limits of the power, he is not entitled to any indemnity.

As regards remuneration, there may be an express term as to remuneration. If not, an attorney will have to rely on an implied contractual term if he is to be paid. It is submitted that if a client appoints a solicitor or an accountant as attorney, there will be an implied right to reasonable remuneration.

If an enduring power has been registered, s 8(2)(b)(iii) EPAA 1985 empowers the court to give directions with regard to the remuneration or expenses of the attorney, whether or not in default of or in accordance with any provision made by the instrument, including directions for the repayment of excessive remuneration, or the payment of additional remuneration.

3. Financial services

Solicitors must comply with the Solicitors' Investment Business Rules 1995. Chapter 5 contains rules which apply to all firms, including rules relating to advertisements and records. Chapter 6 contains the rules which apply to firms undertaking discrete investment business. Chapter 4 defines discrete investment business. It excludes from the definition of discretionary management the situation where no remuneration is received for the discretionary management of investments in addition to any remuneration which may be received for acting as donee of a power of attorney or receiver. The definition of advising excludes the situation where the recommendation is made by a trustee to a co-trustee or attorney to a co-attorney, and no remuneration is received for this in addition to any remuneration which may be received for acting as trustee or attorney. The definitions of dealing and arranging have similar exclusions. There are also exceptions if transaction is carried out through a permitted third party, or the activity is incidental, unless the activity is concerned with packaged products.

4. Miscellaneous points for solicitors

It is understood that claims for negligence arising out of the use of powers of attorney are rare; when they do arise, they are often caused by the use of out-of-date forms. Solicitors acting for the donor of a power, or dealing with the attorney, should ensure that the correct forms have been used.

A solicitor may draft a will for a donor, and the attorney, who may be a relative and possible beneficiary under the will, may ask to see it. If the donor is of full capacity, the permission of the donor for disclosure must be obtained. If the attorney is acting under an enduring power, which has been registered because of the incapacity of the donor, the permission of the Court of Protection should be obtained, unless the power permits disclosure. Solicitors should consider whether the power should contain an express power to disclose the contents of a will.

If a solicitor is instructed by an attorney, the question may arise as to who is the client. Usually it will be the donor of the power.

An attorney under an enduring power cannot consent to medical treatment on behalf of the donor.

A solicitor may be instructed by an attorney acting under an unregistered power. The attorney should be reminded about capacity, and that if the donor lacks capacity, the power should be registered. The attorney should also be advised that an enduring power will be invalid if it has not been registered when it should have been. It may be that the attorney should be asked to give a written assurance, and if there is anything giving rise to suspicion, the instructions of the donor of the power should be sought.

For the purposes of the Solicitors' Accounts Rules, the donor is the solicitor's client where the solicitor is acting under a power of attorney. This means that any money received by the solicitor must be paid into client account. On the other hand, if the solicitor operates the donor's bank account, that is not client's money (see *The Guide to the Professional Conduct of Solicitors 1996* at page 583).

The Law Society have recently published some guidelines for solicitors concerning enduring powers of attorney.

Further guidance can be obtained from the Professional Ethics Division of the Law Society telephone number 0171-242 1222.

Summary

- There may be a contractual duty to act.
- Usually there will be an implied right to remuneration.
- Solicitors may have to comply with the Solicitors' Investment Business Rules 1996.

Chapter 5

Formalities

The Powers of Attorney Act 1971 as amended contains provisions dealing with the formalities required for an ordinary power of attorney. The formalities required for an enduring power of attorney are set out in the Enduring Powers of Attorney Act 1985 ('EPAA 1985'), and the regulations made under that Act. It is therefore necessary to deal separately with the requirements for enduring powers and other powers.

I. Ordinary powers of attorney

1. Individuals

(a) A deed is required

Section 1(1) Powers of Attorney Act 1971, as amended by s 1(8) and Sch 1 Law of Property (Miscellaneous Provisions) Act 1989 ('the 1989 Act') which came into force on 31 July 1990, requires that a power of attorney must be executed as a deed.

Section 1(2) of the 1989 Act provides that an instrument shall not be a deed unless:

(a) it makes it clear on the face of it that it is intended to be a deed by the person making it or, as the case may be, by the parties to it (whether by describing itself as a deed or expressing itself to be executed or signed as a deed or otherwise); and

(b) it is validly executed as a deed by that person or, as the case may be, by one or more of those parties.

(b) Execution of the power by the donor

Section 1(3)(a)(i) of the 1989 Act provides that an instrument is validly executed as a deed by an individual if it is signed by him in the presence of a witness who attests the signature.

(c) Execution of the power by a person on behalf of the donor

It is permissible for the power to be signed by another person, but this must be done at the direction of the donor of the power, and also in his presence. In this situation, two other persons must witness the signing, and they must attest the instrument (s 1(3)(a)(ii) of the 1989 Act).

Under s 1(4) of the 1989 Act 'sign' includes making a mark.

(d) Delivery

Whether the donor of a power signs it himself or not, the power must be delivered by him or a person authorised on his behalf to do so (s 1(3)(b) of the 1989 Act). 'Delivered' in this context means that the donor of the power has shown an intention by acts or words to be bound by the deed. Usually the donor of a power will intend that it should come into effect immediately. If the power is delivered by another person, the authority for this need not be given by deed (s 1(1)(c) of the 1989 Act).

2. Companies

A company granting a power of attorney must use a deed to do so. The law governing the execution of documents by companies was amended by s 130 Companies Act 1989 which inserted a new section into the Companies Act 1985. This new section, s 36A, which came into force on 31 July 1990, provides in subs (2) that a document is executed by a company by the affixing of its common seal. However, subs (3) provides that a company need not have a common seal, and subs (4) provides that a document signed by a director and the secretary of the company, or by two directors, and expressed to be executed by the company has the same effect as if executed under the common seal of the company.

Section 36A(5) provides that if a document makes it clear on the face of it that it is intended to take effect as a deed, it will take effect as a deed on delivery, and there is a rebuttable presumption that it will be delivered on execution.

Section 36A(6) provides that in favour of a purchaser a document will be deemed to have been duly executed by a company if it purports to be signed by a director and the secretary of the company, or by two directors of the company, and, where it makes it clear on its face that it is intended by the person making it to be a deed, to have been delivered upon its being executed. 'Purchaser' is defined as the purchaser in good faith for valuable consideration and includes a lessee, mortgagee or other person who for valuable consideration acquires an interest in property. Thus a purchaser who knows or suspects that the execution is defective will not be protected.

If the company affixes its seal to a power, s 74(1) Law of Property Act 1925 provides that in favour of a purchaser a deed will be deemed to have been duly executed by a company if its seal is affixed to it in the presence of and attested by its clerk, secretary or other permanent officer or his deputy, and a member of the board of directors, council or other governing body of the company. Furthermore, where a seal purporting to be the seal of the company has been affixed to a deed, attested by persons holding those offices, the deed will be deemed to have been executed in accordance with the requirements of the section, and to take effect accordingly. 'Purchaser' is defined in s 205(1)(xxi) Law of Property Act 1925 as a purchaser in good faith for valuable consideration and includes a lessee, mortgagee or other person who for valuable consideration acquires an interest in property. Again a purchaser who suspects or knows that the execution is defective will not be protected.

II. Enduring powers of attorney

Unlike other powers of attorney, an enduring power of attorney can survive the mental incapacity of the donor, and as a consequence the EPAA 1985 lays down special rules for enduring powers.

Section 2(1) EPAA 1985 requires an enduring power to:

(a) be in a prescribed form;

(b) be executed in a prescribed manner by the donor and the attorney; and

(c) incorporate at the time of execution by the donor the prescribed explanatory information.

1. Form

The Lord Chancellor is empowered to make regulations as to the form and execution of instruments creating powers of attorney, and s 2(2)(a) EPAA 1985 requires these regulations to contain whatever provisions are appropriate to ensure that every enduring power of attorney contains information in a prescribed form explaining the general effect of creating or accepting an enduring power. Section 2(2)(b) EPAA 1985 provides that the power must also contain statements:

  (i) by the donor, that he intends the power to continue in spite of any intervening mental incapacity;

 (ii) by the donor that he read or had read to him the information explaining the effect of creating the power;

(iii) by the attorney that he understands the duty of registration imposed by the Act.

The Enduring Powers of Attorney (Prescribed Form) Regulations 1990 (SI 1990 No 1376) ('EPR'), replacing regulations made in 1987 which had in turn replaced regulations made in 1986, came into force on 31 July 1990. Regulation 2(1) EPR provides that an enduring power must be in the form set out in the Schedule to the regulations. The usual practice is to obtain printed forms from law stationers, but they can be typed, or produced by word processor. Readers are referred to the form, and their attention is drawn to the following points, some of which are raised in articles by PD Lewis in *The Law Society's Gazette* (26 November 1986 at page 3566 and 29 April 1987 at page 1219):

(a) The enduring power must contain all the explanatory information headed 'About using this form' in Part A of the Schedule and all the relevant marginal notes to Parts B and C. It may also include such additions (including paragraph numbers) or restrictions as the donor may decide (reg 2(1) EPR). The explanatory information may be bound up with the power, or stapled to it. (See Practice Direction [1989] 2 All ER 64.)

Section 2(5) EPAA 1985 provides that an instrument in the prescribed form purporting to have been executed in the prescribed manner will be taken, in the absence of evidence to the contrary, to be a document which incorporated at the time of execution by the donor the prescribed explanatory information. There is thus a rebuttable presumption that the explanatory notes were attached to the power in the prescribed form.

(b) Although it is clearly desirable that the full name of the donor should be inserted, it is not fatal to an application for registration of the power that the donor's middle name or names have been omitted. Affidavit evidence will be required.

(c) The omission of the donor's date of birth, or the insertion of an incorrect date, will not normally be fatal to an application for registration. An affidavit exhibiting the donor's birth certificate will be required.

(d) Regulation 2(2)(a)(i) EPR provides that where the donor appoints only one attorney, everything between the square brackets on the first page of Part B will be excluded either by omission or deletion.

(e) It is possible to appoint joint attorneys, an alternative attorney and the senior partner in a firm of solicitors; these possibilities are discussed later in this chapter.

(f) Where there are alternatives, one and only one of any pair of alternatives must be excluded, again either by omission or deletion (reg 2(2)(a)(ii) EPR).

(g) If two or more attorneys are appointed, either the words 'jointly' or 'jointly and severally' must be deleted. If one is not deleted, the power will not be an enduring power because of s 11(1) EPAA 1985.

(h) 'all my property and affairs' and 'the following property and affairs': omission of both these alternatives is a material difference, and will render the power invalid as an enduring power.

(i) The omission of the statement by the donor that he or she intends the power to continue even if he or she becomes mentally incapable is a material difference.

(j) Regulation 2(2)(b) EPR provides that there may also be excluded either by omission or deletion:

    (i) the words on the second page of Part B 'subject to the following restrictions and conditions', if those words do not apply;

    (ii) the attestation details for a second witness in Parts B and C if a second witness is not required; and

    (iii) any marginal notes which correspond with any words excluded under the provisions of this paragraph and the two notes numbered 1 and 2 which appear immediately under the heading to Part C.

It is permissible for an enduring power to be produced on a word processor leaving out the alternatives.

2. Execution

(a) Execution by donor and attorney

Regulation 3(1) EPR provides that an enduring power of attorney must be executed:

(a)   by both the donor and the attorney; and

(b)   in the presence of a witness, who

(c)   must sign the form and give his full name and address.

The signature can be typed, in block capitals or made by means of a rubber stamp (see PD Lewis in *The Law Society's Gazette* (26 November 1986 at page 3567)).

The donor and the attorney need not sign at the same time, and they need not sign in the presence of the same witness. But reg 3(2) EPR provides that a donor and an attorney must not witness the signature of each other nor one attorney the signature of another.

(b) Execution by a person on behalf of donor

Regulation 3(3) EPR permits the power to be executed at the direction of the donor, provided the following requirements are satisfied:

(a)   it must be signed in the presence of two witnesses who shall each sign the form and give their full names and addresses; and

(b)   a statement that the enduring power of attorney has been executed at the direction of the donor must be inserted in Part B;

(c)   it must not be signed by an attorney or any of the witnesses to the signature of either the donor or an attorney.

Under reg 2(3)(b) EPR the form of execution by the donor may be adapted where the enduring power of attorney is executed at the direction of the donor.

(c) Execution by a person on behalf of donee

Regulation 3(4) EPR permits an enduring power to be executed at the direction of an attorney, provided the following conditions are satisfied:

(a)   it must be signed in the presence of two witnesses who must each sign the form and give their full names and addresses; and

(b) a statement that the enduring power of attorney has been executed at the direction of the attorney must be inserted in Part C;

(c) it must not be signed by either the donor, an attorney or any of the witnesses to the signature of either the donor or an attorney.

If a trust corporation is appointed attorney, the form of execution by an attorney may be adapted to provide for execution by a trust corporation.

The following points should also be noted:

(a) The donor must execute the power before the attorney.

(b) The attorney should execute the power as soon as possible after it has been executed by the donor in case the donor becomes incapable of managing his or her affairs in the meantime, or the power is registered. Execution by the attorney would then be too late. (See page 10 of *Enduring Powers of Attorney* published by the Public Trust Office.)

(c) If the attorney's signature was not witnessed when he or she first signed it, there is doubt about whether the attorney can re-execute the document; in any event if the donor has become mentally incapable, any re-execution will be ineffective. If the only defect is that the witness failed to give his or her name, address or occupation, this can be cured by means of an affidavit.

(d) Although a spouse can witness the signature of the donor, it is suggested that this is not desirable as it may not be possible to compel a spouse to give evidence in proceedings relating to the power, and may lead to family friction.

(e) It is not a material difference to omit the address or occupation of a witness.

(f) It is not a material difference to omit the dates when the donor or attorney signed.

These points are discussed by PD Lewis in *The Law Society's Gazette* (26 November 1986, page 3566 and 29 April 1987, page 1219); see also Chapter 7.

Alterations and deletions do not have to be initialled: PD Lewis, *The Law Society's Gazette* (28 October 1987 at page 3084) and *Enduring Powers of Attorney* published by the Public Trust Office.

3. Blind or physically handicapped donors

Blind or physically handicapped donors or attorneys can make a mark, and reg 2(3) EPR provides that the form of execution by the donor or by an attorney may be adapted in such a case. Additional words should be added to the attestation clause to show that the notes in Part A of the prescribed form have been read to the donor and that he or she understood them. The attorney may become under a duty to apply for registration of the power (this is discussed in Chapter 7). If this is the case, the court will require an explanation of how notification was given to the donor of the intention to apply for registration (see PD Lewis, *The Law Society's Gazette* (26 November 1986, page 3567 and 29 April 1987, page 1220) and *Enduring Powers of Attorney* published by the Public Trust Office).

4. Joint powers and joint and several powers

It is possible to appoint more than one attorney under an enduring power, but they must be appointed to act jointly or jointly and severally (s 11(1) EPAA 1985). A joint power means that all the attorneys must join in making decisions, whereas if the power is joint and several, one attorney can bind the others.

In the case of joint and several powers, at least one of the attorneys must execute the power, but if the power is registered (see Chapter 7), or the donor becomes mentally incapable, only those attorneys who have executed the power can act (reg 4 EPR). One attorney cannot witness the signature of another (reg 3(2) EPR).

As mentioned earlier in this chapter, if two or more persons are appointed attorneys, either the words 'jointly' or 'jointly and severally' in the prescribed form must be deleted.

Section 11(4), which applies to joint and several powers (s 11(3)), provides that a failure, as respects any one attorney, to comply with the requirements for the creation of enduring powers, will prevent the instrument creating such a power in his case without, however, affecting its efficacy for that purpose as respects the other or others or its efficacy in his case for the purpose of creating a power of attorney which is not an enduring power. Thus if one joint and several attorney fails to comply with the rules for enduring powers, the power can still be an enduring power as regards those attorneys who do comply, and it can operate as an ordinary power for those who do not comply.

5. Alternative appointments

It is permissible to appoint one person with the proviso that if he or she does not act, another person is to be the attorney. Although s 11(1) EPAA 1985 provides that an instrument which appoints more than one person to be an attorney cannot create an enduring power unless the attorneys are appointed to act jointly or jointly and severally, the court takes the view that an alternative appointment is in fact the appointment of one person (PD Lewis, *The Law Society's Gazette* (26 November 1986 at page 3567) and *Enduring Powers of Attorney* issued by the Public Trust Office); but s 2(9) EPAA 1985 provides that a power of attorney which gives the attorney, or if it is a joint attorney, any attorney, the right to appoint a substitute or successor cannot be an enduring power (Sch 3 Pt I para 2 EPAA 1985).

6. Alterations to the prescribed form

It is essential to be very careful about alterations to the prescribed form of an enduring power.

Section 2(6) EPAA 1985 provides that an enduring power will be treated as sufficient in point of form and expression if it differs only in an immaterial respect from the prescribed form.

Regulation 2(1) EPR provides that all the explanatory information headed 'About using this form' in Part A of the Schedule and all relevant marginal notes to Parts B and C must be included.

Regulation 2(2) EPR permits certain omissions and deletions, including the omission or deletion of one and only one of any pair of alternatives, and reg 2(2)(b)(iii) provides that any marginal notes corresponding with any words excluded under the provisions of that paragraph may also be excluded.

What else constitutes an immaterial difference? In articles in *The Law Society's Gazette* (26 November 1986 at page 3566 and 29 April 1987 at page 1219) PD Lewis, Assistant Public Trustee, offered some guidance, although the rules were then contained in regulations made in 1986. According to the articles, the following differences are considered to be immaterial:

- omission of the donor's date of birth;
- omission of the address of a witness;
- omission of the dates when the donor or attorney signed;
- omission of donor's middle names;

- donor's signature witnessed by wife of attorney;
- explanatory information bound up with the power or stapled to it.

It may be necessary to file affidavit evidence about these omissions. According to PD Lewis, the following differences are material:

- not deleting 'jointly' or 'jointly and severally';
- omission of both alternatives 'all my property and affairs' and 'the following property and affairs';
- omission of the statement by the donor that he intends the power to continue in spite of his supervening incapacity.

Regulation 2(4) states that, subject to paras (1), (2) and (3) of reg 2 and to reg 4, an enduring power of attorney which seeks to exclude any provision contained in the Regulations is not a valid enduring power of attorney.

It is clearly best to amend, omit or delete parts of the prescribed form as little as possible, and in any event any alteration should be within the limits of the EPAA 1985 and the EPR.

7. Miscellaneous points

- It is in order to appoint 'the senior partner in the firm of ...'.
- An attorney living out of the jurisdiction can be appointed, but if this caused problems when the power was registered, the court might appoint a receiver.
- It is probable that a donor living abroad can grant an enduring power.

See PD Lewis, *The Law Society's Gazette* (26 November 1986 at page 3568).

8. Non-compliance with formalities

Section 9(6) EPAA 1985 deals with the situation where an instrument has failed to create a valid enduring power, and the power has been revoked by the donor's mental incapacity. In his article in *The Law Society's Gazette* (26 November 1986) PD Lewis states at page 3567:

'A power which has not been executed by the attorney cannot be an enduring power but may be used as an ordinary power unless and until the donor loses capacity.'

It would thus seem to be clear that an invalid enduring power can take effect as an ordinary power. However, RT Oerton in an article in the *Solicitors' Journal* (11 December 1987 at pages 1645 and 1646) has argued that an invalid enduring power can only take effect as an ordinary power in very limited circumstances. The author argues that most enduring powers will be general powers, and that the donee will have the powers conferred by s 3 EPAA 1985. If the enduring power is invalid, the donee cannot have these powers. Furthermore, the author argues that the invalid enduring power cannot take effect as an ordinary power within s 10 Powers of Attorney Act 1971, because it is not in the form prescribed by that section. Additionally, it is argued that it cannot take effect as a general power outside s 10 Powers of Attorney Act 1971 because it was necessary to use a much longer form of power of attorney to confer general powers on an attorney before the passing of the 1971 Act. There is also the question of intention: the donor intends to create an enduring power, not an ordinary power. In the light of all these factors, the author concludes that an invalid limited enduring power may be valid as an ordinary power, but not an invalid general enduring power.

There is clearly considerable force in these arguments. However, it is submitted that although, in the past, powers of attorney were long, it may be that they were unnecessarily lengthy, and that a shorter version would have sufficed. Thus an enduring power which is invalid under s 3 EPAA 1985 can perhaps operate outside the Powers of Attorney Act 1971.

As there is clearly some doubt about whether an invalid enduring power can take effect as an ordinary power, the wisest course of action is to assume that it cannot.

Summary

1. Ordinary powers of attorney

(a) Individuals

- The power must be signed by the donor of the power in the presence of a witness who attests the signature.
- Alternatively, it can be signed by another individual at his direction and in his presence and the presence of two witnesses who each attest the signature.
- The power must be delivered as a deed by him or a person authorised to do so on his behalf; this authority can be given orally, although it is desirable that it should be in writing.

(b) Companies

- A company can affix its seal to a power. The secretary and a director must be present and attest the power.

- A company need not affix its seal to a power. A director and the secretary of a company or two directors can execute a power of attorney on behalf of the company, provided it is expressed to be executed by the company.

- The power should make it clear on its face that it is intended to be a deed; the easiest way of achieving this is to indicate that it is executed or signed as a deed at the place where the seal of the company is affixed, or the document is signed.

2. Enduring powers of attorney

- The prescribed form must be used.

- Comply strictly with the explanatory notes; it is unwise to alter the prescribed form.

- The power must be executed by both the donor and the donee in the presence of a witness who must sign the form and give his or her full name and address.

- The form can be executed at the direction of the donor and the donee provided it is signed in the presence of two witnesses who must each sign the form and give their full names and addresses. The form must be amended to indicate that it has been signed at the direction of the donor or attorney.

Chapter 6

Duration and termination of powers of attorney

This chapter deals with the circumstances in which a power of attorney will come to an end. It is necessary to distinguish between ordinary powers of attorney and enduring powers of attorney as although the rules are similar, there are substantial differences in some areas.

I. Ordinary powers of attorney

1. Expiry

Many powers of attorney are granted without any limitation as to time. However, a power of attorney may be granted for a specified period, and once that period has expired, the donee's authority ceases. If the period is specified by reference to months, s 61 Law of Propety Act 1925 provides that 'month' means calendar month unless the context otherwise requires.

A power may also expire even though no time limit is specified. In *Danby v Coutts & Co* (1885) 29 Ch D 500 the donor appointed two attorneys. Although there was nothing in the main part of the power about its duration, a recital stated that the donor was about to return to South Australia, and that the donor wanted to appoint attorneys to act for him whilst he was abroad. It was held that the recital controlled the main part of the document, and that the power was exercisable only whilst the donor was abroad.

It should be noted that s 25(1) Trustee Act 1925 as amended by the Powers of Attorney Act 1971 permits trustees to delegate the powers and discretions vested in them for a period not exceeding twelve months. In addition, s 9(1) Trusts of Land and Appointment of Trustees Act 1996 (which came into force on 1 January 1997) permits delegation by trustees of land to beneficiaries for any period or indefinitely. The capacity of trustees to delegate is discussed in Chapter 9.

2. Performance of purpose of power

Although powers of attorney frequently give the donee a wide authority to act for the donor of the power, often to do anything the donor could have lawfully done, the power may be limited, and may give authority to the donee to complete only one transaction. For example, the authority may be limited to the acts necessary to complete the sale of a particular property. As soon as the sale of that property has been completed, the authority of the donee of the power ceases.

An example of the termination of an ordinary agency by the performance of the purpose is provided by the case of *Gillow & Co v Aberdare* (1892) 9 TLR 12. The plaintiffs were agents, and they were instructed to let a house furnished or unfurnished, or to sell the ground lease. The plaintiffs successfully negotiated the letting of the property to a Mr Tooth, and were paid commission. Mr Tooth then bought the ground lease, but he conducted the negotiations through another agent. It was held that the plaintiffs were not entitled to any commission on the sale of the ground lease as their agency had terminated on completion of the letting to Mr Tooth.

A power of attorney authorising the donee to let or sell a property may thus terminate if the donee lets the property. If it is intended that the donee should have the power both to let and sell the property after letting, it should be clearly stated in the power that this is the case.

3. Express revocation

In *Bromley v Holland* (1802) 7 Ves 3 Lord Eldon LC stated at page 28 that a power of attorney was a 'revocable instrument', and so the donor can revoke it at any time, unless it is an irrevocable power. The revocation can be oral, in writing or by deed (*The Margaret Mitchell* (1888) Swab 382, 166 ER 1174), but it is ineffective until it is received by the donee (*Re Oriental Bank Corporation, ex parte Guillemin* (1884) 28 Ch D 634). Notice to one joint attorney is effective (*Bristow and Porter v Taylor* (1817) 2 Stark 50, 171 ER 568).

If it is an irrevocable power, the donor will not be able to revoke it without the consent of the donee. Irrevocable powers are usually granted in commercial transactions, and are discussed later in this chapter and in Chapter 12.

Often the donee of the power is a solicitor; if the solicitor is given a power which is expressed to last for a specified period, can the donor terminate it before the end of that specified period? The answer is yes, but if there was a contract not to terminate it for the specified period, the solicitor might be able to sue for damages for breach of contract. Whether the solicitor can sue depends on the terms of the contract with the client; usually it is only the express terms which can be considered as the courts are very reluctant to imply any terms into the contract. In *Hamlyn & Co v Wood & Co* [1891] 2 QB 485 CA Lord Esher MR said:

> 'I have for a long time understood that the Court has no right to imply in a written contract any such stipulation, unless on considering the terms of the contract in a reasonable and business manner, an implication necessarily arises that the parties must have intended that the suggested stipulation should exist. It is not enough to say that it would be a reasonable thing to make such an implication.'

If no period for the duration of the contract is specified, the courts will be reluctant to imply any term that the contract is to last for a set term, and it will usually be terminable by, at the very most, reasonable notice. In *Martin-Baker Aircraft Co Ltd v Canadian Flight Equipment Ltd* [1955] 2 QB 556 the subject matter of the dispute were contracts with no or limited provision for termination. It was held that they were terminable on notice. McNair J, at pages 577 and 578, said:

> 'Accordingly, it appears to me that I have to approach the determination of this question not with any presumption in favour of permanence; and, indeed, if there is any presumption at all, it would seem to me to be a presumption the other way ...
>
> The common law, in applying the law merchant to commercial transactions, has always proceeded on the basis of reasonableness in filling up the gaps in a contract which the parties have made on the basis of what is reasonable, so far as that does not conflict with the express terms of the contract, rather than on the basis of rigidity ...
>
> It is, of course, true that this kind of consideration can in many cases be excluded by express provision; but where the contract leaves the matter open, I think that the common law approach would be to provide a solution which is reasonable.'

Thus, whether or not the duration of the power of attorney is specified, in the absence of any specified agreement between the solicitor and the client as to how long the solicitor is to operate the power, the client will usually be able to terminate both the power and the contract, at the most on giving reasonable notice, without breaking the contract, unless it is one of the few situations when the court would be prepared to imply a term as to the duration of the contract.

It is essential that notice that the power has been revoked should be given to anyone who might rely on it. This is because s 5(2) Powers of Attorney Act 1971 provides that where a power of attorney has been revoked and a person, without knowledge of the revocation, deals with the donee of the power, the transaction between them shall, in favour of that person, be as valid as if the power had then been in existence. It is not good enough to destroy the original, or to note on it that it has been revoked, as a copy can be used to prove the contents of an instrument under s 3(1) Powers of Attorney Act 1971. (See *Powers of Attorney* (Longman, 8th edition, 1991) by Aldridge at page 57.)

A donee acting under a power of attorney warrants that he had authority to act under the power, and if that authority does not exist, the donee may be liable in damages to anyone who suffers loss as a result of relying on that warranty (*Starkey v Bank of England* [1903] AC 114 HL). However, s 5(1) Powers of Attorney Act 1971 may protect an attorney in this situation. It provides that a donee of a power of attorney who acts in pursuance of a power at a time when it has been revoked will not, by reason of the revocation, incur any liability (either to the donor or to any other person) if at that time he did not know that the power had been revoked. These matters are discussed further in Chapters 11 and 12.

The donee is also liable to the donor if he continues to act knowing that a power has been revoked (*Pearson v Graham* (1837) 6 A & E 899, 112 ER 344).

4. Implied revocation

Any act by the donor inconsistent with the continuance of the power will have the effect of revoking the power, unless it is irrevocable. For example, if a donee is given a power of attorney authorising the sale of a particular property at a specified price, and the donor signs a contract for the sale of the property at a higher price, this is an act inconsistent with the power of attorney, and has the effect of revoking it (*Smith v Jennings* Lane 97, 145 ER 329). However a donee is entitled to assume that the power of attorney is still in existence until the donor does some act inconsistent with the power (*Re Oriental Bank Corporation ex parte Guillemin* (1884) 28 Ch D 634).

As with express revocation, a person dealing with the donee without knowledge of the revocation is protected by s 5(2).

A donee acting under a power which has been revoked will be liable in damages for breach of warranty of authority. However, s 5(1) Powers of Attorney Act 1971 protects the donee of a power who acts in pursuance of a power at a time when it has been revoked if at that time the donee did not know that the power had been revoked.

A donee who continues to act under a power knowing that it has been impliedly revoked will be liable to the donor.

5. Bankruptcy

(a) The donor

The bankruptcy of the donor of a power of attorney revokes the power (*Markwick v Hardingham* (1880) 15 Ch D 339 CA) unless it is irrevocable, but the donee will still have authority to complete the formalities of a transaction entered into before the bankruptcy (see *Halsbury's Laws of England*, 4th edition, volume 1(2) paragraph 199).

At what stage in the bankruptcy is the power revoked? Section 284 Insolvency Act 1986 provides that any disposition made during the period beginning with the day of the presentation of the petition and ending with the vesting of the bankrupt's property in a trustee is void except to the extent that it is or was made with the consent of the court, or is or was subsequently ratified by the court. Under s 284(2) a similar rule is applied to a payment whether in cash or otherwise.

As any disposition of property by a bankrupt is void in the period beginning with the presentation of the bankruptcy petition, any power of attorney granted by the bankrupt will terminate on the presentation of the petition.

Section 284(4) provides that 'the preceding provisions of this section do not give a remedy against any person –

(a) in respect of any property or payment which he received before the commencement of the bankruptcy in good faith, for value and without notice that the petition had been presented, or

(b) in respect of any interest in property which derives from an interest in respect of which there is, by virtue of this subsection, no remedy.'

Presumably this section would operate to protect a purchaser from the attorney of a donor who has become bankrupt, provided the purchaser acted in good faith and without notice that the petition had been presented.

It is also possible for debtors to enter into voluntary arrangements with their creditors (ss 252–263 Insolvency Act 1986). It is submitted that if a donor of a power enters into a voluntary arrangement with his creditors, it will not cause the power of attorney to terminate unless the continuance of the power is inconsistent with the voluntary arrangement. For example, if the debtor grants a general power of attorney, a voluntary arrangement providing that the debtor's business should not be sold would revoke the power as far as the business was concerned.

There is further protection in the Powers of Attorney Act 1971 for persons dealing with the attorney without knowledge of the revocation. As mentioned earlier, under s 5(2) a person dealing with the donee of the power without knowledge of the revocation will be protected, but the donee may be liable for breach of warranty of authority, although he or she may be able to claim the protection of s 5(1).

(b) The donee

The bankruptcy of the donee of a power of attorney does not automatically terminate the power. It will do so if the continuation of the power is inconsistent with the bankruptcy (*Bailey v Thurston & Co Ltd* [1903] 1 KB 137 CA). The situation is the same if the donee enters into a voluntary arrangement with his creditors.

6. Insolvency of a company

(a) The donor company

If a company grants a power of attorney, and is then wound up, the power will be revoked. However, the donee of the power will still be able to complete the formalities required for a transaction entered into before the revocation.

Section 86 Insolvency Act 1986 provides that 'a voluntary winding up is deemed to commence at the time of the passing of the resolution for voluntary winding up', and s 87(1) provides that as from the commencement of the winding up the company shall cease to carry on business, except so far as may be required for its beneficial winding up. It could be argued that a power of attorney granted by a company could be exercised for the limited purpose specified in s 87(1), but, having regard to s 127, it is unwise to rely on this argument.

Section 127 deals with a winding up by the court, and provides that in such proceedings 'any disposition of the company's property ... made after the commencement of the winding up is, unless the court otherwise orders, void'. Section 129(1) provides that 'if, before the presentation of a petition for the winding up of a company by the court, a resolution has been passed by the company for voluntary winding up, the winding up of the company is deemed to have commenced at the time of the passing of the resolution; and unless the court, on proof of fraud or mistake, directs otherwise, all proceedings taken in the voluntary winding up are deemed to have been validly taken'. Subsection (2) provides that 'in any other case, the winding up ... is deemed to commence at the time of the presentation of the petition for winding up'.

Thus it seems that a power of attorney cannot continue once a resolution for winding up the company has been passed, or a petition for the winding up of the company has been presented to the court.

Action short of winding up may be taken against a company in financial difficulties. Under the Insolvency Act 1986 the following courses of action are available in respect of such a company:

  (i) a voluntary arrangement (ss 1–7 Insolvency Act 1986);
 (ii) an administration order (ss 8–27 Insolvency Act 1986);
(iii) the appointment of a receiver or administrative receiver (ss 28–72 Insolvency Act 1986).

Will these events revoke the power? It is submitted that the power will be revoked only if the continuance of the power is consistent with the consequences of any of the actions which can be taken by or against the company.

Entering into a voluntary arrangement, or making an administration order, or appointing an administrative receiver is not necessarily inconsistent with the continuance of a power of attorney granted by the company. However, in so far as it is inconsistent, any power will be revoked; for example, if a voluntary arrangement provided that certain property should not be sold, any power of attorney authorising the attorney to sell it would be revoked to that extent.

If the power of attorney is coupled with an interest, it may not be revocable. In *Sowman v David Samuel Trust Ltd* [1978] 1 WLR 22 the company granted a debenture in favour of two banks, which authorised them to appoint a receiver, and appointed the banks and any person appointed by them attorney for the company. The banks appointed a receiver, and the company then went into liquidation. Subsequently, the receiver agreed to sell a property to the second plaintiff. The conveyance was executed by the banks and the receiver. It was held that the conveyance was effective. Goulding J said at page 30:

> 'Winding-up deprives the receiver, under such a debenture as that now in suit, of power to bind the company personally by acting as its agent. It does not in the least affect his powers to hold and dispose of the company's property comprised in the debenture, including his power to use the company's name for that purpose, for such powers are given by the disposition of the company's property which it made (in equity) by the debenture itself. That disposition is binding on the company and those claiming through it, as well in liquidation as before liquidation, except of course where the debenture … is otherwise invalidated by some provision of law applicable to the winding-up.'

It was also held that the power of attorney had not been revoked. Goulding J said at page 30:

> 'It is clear law that in their hands it was not revoked by the winding-up of the company. The conclusion rests on a double foundation: first, the common law rule tritely expressed in the phrase that "an authority coupled with an interest is irrevocable" and, secondly, the statutory enactment in section 4 of the Powers of Attorney Act 1971. By the conveyance of March 4, 1977, the debenture holders used their power of attorney to execute the assurance required to complete a sale validly effected by the receiver for the purposes of the security.'

Section 4 Powers of Attorney Act 1971 is discussed in Chapter 12.

Section 5(2) Powers of Attorney Act 1971 protects any person dealing with the donee of the power without knowledge of its revocation, and s 5(1) may protect the donee.

(b) The donee company

If a company is a donee, it is submitted that the power is revoked as soon as a resolution for the winding up of the company has been passed, or a petition for the winding up of the company has been presented to the court, because s 87(1) Insolvency Act 1986 provides that the company must cease to carry on business as from the commencement of the winding up, except in so far as may be required for its beneficial winding up; this provision is discussed above. If a donee company enters into a voluntary arrangement, or an administration order is made, or a receiver is appointed, the power of attorney will terminate if its continuance is inconsistent with the effects of any of these events.

7. Death

The death of the donor or donee of a power terminates a power of attorney, unless it is irrevocable. However, the personal representatives of a deceased donor may be able to ratify a contract entered into after the death of the donor (*Foster v Bates* (1843) 12 M & W 226).

If two or more attorneys are appointed jointly, the death of one will cause the power to terminate (*Adams v Buckland* (1705) 2 Vern 514, 23 ER 929); but if the authority of the attorneys is joint and several, the death of one attorney will not affect the authority of the other(s) who can continue to exercise the power.

Section 5(2) Powers of Attorney Act 1971 applies to protect any person dealing with the donee without knowledge of the death of the donor, and s 5(1) may protect the donee.

8. Disclaimer of power

The donee of a power of attorney can disclaim the power. The donee must give notice to the donor, and the notice will be ineffective until received by the donor (*Re Oriental Bank Corporation, ex parte Guillemin* (1884) 28 Ch D 634). The notice can be written or oral (*The Margaret Mitchell* (1888) Swab 382, 166 ER 1174). However, it may be that there is a contractual relationship between the donor and the donee, for example if the donee is a solicitor or accountant, and an unjustified disclaimer might amount to a breach of contract.

9. Mental incapacity

The mental incapacity of the donor or donee of a power terminates the power (*Drew v Nunn* [1879] 4 QBD 661 CA), unless it is an irrevocable power.

Section 5(2) Powers of Attorney Act 1971 protects the person dealing with the donee without knowledge of the revocation, and s 5(1) may protect the donee.

10. Illegality

If the performance of a power of attorney necessarily involves the commission of an illegal act, the power will terminate. For example, if the donor of the power becomes an enemy, the authority conferred by the power may cease. According to Cozens-Hardy MR in *Tingley v Muller* [1917] 2 Ch 144 CA at page 156:

> '... "enemy" means any person resident or carrying on business in an enemy country, but does not include persons of enemy nationality who are neither resident nor carrying on business in the enemy country.'

Thus even if the donor and donee become 'enemies', the power of attorney will not terminate if neither resides nor carries on business in the enemy country.

Even if the donor has become an enemy as defined above, a transaction authorised by a power granted before the donor became an enemy may be valid. In *Tingley*, the defendant, a German by birth, executed an irrevocable power of attorney in May 1915 whilst he was resident in this country. He then travelled to Germany under a government permit. It was held that the power was still valid even though the defendant had become an alien enemy. The attorney could complete the transaction without consulting the defendant, and the proceeds of sale would be retained in this country.

In *Hangkam Kwintong Woo v Lin Lan Fong* [1951] 2 All ER 567 the donor of a power of attorney lived in Hong Kong, which at the time was occupied by the Japanese. He left Hong Kong, and went to live in Free China. The donee of the power sold a house belonging to the attorney. It was held that the power was still in existence as it did not involve any trading with the enemy.

11. Irrevocable powers

It may be that the donor and donee will want to create a power of attorney which cannot be revoked. Irrevocable powers are usually found in commercial arrangements. For example, mortgages sometimes give the mortgagee a power of attorney authorising the mortgagee to deal with the mortgaged property. A vendor may also give a purchaser a power of attorney to transfer property if the purchaser does not intend to take a conveyance of the property, for example if it is a sale to a home relocation company. A mortgagee or purchaser in these situations would not want the power to be revoked. The Powers of Attorney Act 1971 recognises this, and contains special provisions dealing with powers which are part of a commercial arrangement and which are intended to continue in spite of events which would normally cause a revocation.

Section 4(1) Powers of Attorney Act 1971 provides:

'Where a power of attorney is expressed to be irrevocable and is given to secure –

(a)   a proprietary interest of the donee of the power; or

(b)   the performance of an obligation owed to the donee, then, so long as the donee has that interest or the obligation remains undischarged, the power shall not be revoked –

    (i) by the donor without the consent of the donee; or

    (ii) by the death, incapacity or bankruptcy of the donor or, if the donor is a body corporate, by its winding up or dissolution.'

This subsection is clearly wide enough to cover all the situations mentioned above. Furthermore, the section protects subsequent owners of the proprietary interest. Section 4(2) states:

'A power of attorney given to secure a proprietary interest may be given to the person entitled to the interest and persons deriving title under him to that interest, and those persons shall be duly constituted donees of the power for all purposes of the power but without prejudice to any right to appoint substitutes given by the power.'

Section 4 and the protection available to third parties are discussed in Chapter 12.

II. Enduring powers of attorney

1. Expiry

The principles appear to be the same as for ordinary powers of attorney. Section 3(1) Enduring Powers of Attorney Act 1985 ('EPAA 1985') states that an enduring power may be conferred subject to conditions and restrictions, and reg 2(1) Enduring Powers of Attorney (Prescribed Form) Regulations 1990 (SI 1990

No 1376) provides that the prescribed form may include such additions or restrictions as the donor may decide.

Under s 4(1) EPAA 1985, if the attorney has reason to believe that the donor is becoming mentally incapable, the attorney must as soon as practicable make an application to the court for the registration of the instrument creating the power (for details of the provisions relating to registration of enduring powers, see Chapter 7).

Section 8(4)(d) EPAA 1985 provides that the court will cancel the registration of an enduring power on being satisfied that the power has expired. The procedure for cancelling the registration of enduring powers is discussed in Chapter 7.

2. Performance of purpose of power

The principles are the same as for ordinary powers. Section 3(1) EPAA 1985 and the prescribed form permit a general or limited authority to be conferred; if authority is given for one transaction, the authority conferred by that power will terminate when that transaction has been completed.

Section (8)(4)(d) EPAA 1985 applies to this situation (see above), and so the court must cancel the registration of a power on being satisfied that the purpose has been fulfilled.

3. Express revocation

The principle that a power of attorney can be revoked at any time still applies, but the EPAA 1985 has in effect modified this rule.

Under s 7(1) EPAA 1985, once a power is registered, any revocation of the power by the donor must be confirmed by the court. However, until registration, no confirmation by the court is necessary. Under s 8(3) the court must confirm the revocation of the power if satisfied that the donor has done whatever is necessary in law to effect an express revocation of the power, and was mentally capable of revoking the power of attorney when he did so (regardless of his mental capability when the court considers the application). Under s 8(4)(a) the court must cancel the registration on confirming the revocation. The procedure for cancelling a power is discussed in Chapter 7.

Subsections 5(1) and 5(2) Powers of Attorney Act 1971 may operate to protect the donee and person dealing with the donee. These provisions are discussed in more detail above and in Chapter 12.

4. Implied revocation

Until registration, any act by the donor inconsistent with the power will revoke it, but after registration ss 7(1) and 8(3) and (4) EPAA 1985 apply, so that once the power is registered, any revocation must be confirmed by the court. Section 8(3) and (4) apply only to express revocation; thus after registration of an enduring power, the donor must expressly revoke the power.

Section 5(1) and (2) Powers of Attorney Act 1971 may protect the donee and persons dealing with the attorney.

5. Bankruptcy

As with ordinary powers, the bankruptcy of the donor of the power will revoke the power. Although in the case of ordinary powers the bankruptcy of the donee may not necessarily revoke the power, under s 2(10) EPAA 1985 the bankruptcy of the donee of an enduring power will revoke the power whatever the circumstances of the bankruptcy.

If it is a joint power, the bankruptcy of any attorney will revoke the power (Sch 3 Pt I para 2 EPAA 1985), but if it is a joint and several power, only the bankruptcy of the last remaining attorney under the power will cause a revocation. The bankruptcy of any other attorney under a joint and several power causes that person to cease to be an attorney whatever the circumstances of the bankruptcy (Sch 3 Pt II para 7 EPAA 1985).

Section 8(4)(d) EPAA 1985 provides that the court will cancel the registration of the power if it is satisfied that the power has been revoked by the bankruptcy of the donor or donee of the power. Section 11(7), which applies to joint and several attorneys, provides that the court or the Public Trustee will not cancel the registration of an instrument under s 8(4) for any of the causes vitiating registration specified in that subsection if an enduring power subsists as respects some attorney who is not affected thereby, but will give effect to it by the prescribed qualification of the registration. Thus if one joint and several attorney becomes bankrupt, the court will not cancel the registration, but will amend it. Readers are referred to Chapter 7 for a discussion of the procedural requirements for cancellation.

A voluntary arrangement may have the effect of revoking a power; the EPAA 1985 does not deal specifically with what happens in this situation, but presumably it takes effect as an express revocation of the power.

Section 5(1) and (2) Powers of Attorney Act 1971, may operate to protect the donee and persons dealing with the attorney.

6. Insolvency of a trust corporation appointed as attorney

As with ordinary powers, the winding up or dissolution of a trust corporation will revoke any power of attorney given to the company, and s 8(4)(d) EPAA 1985 provides that the court will cancel the registration of an enduring power of attorney on being satisfied that a body corporate appointed as an attorney has been wound up or dissolved. For a discussion of the procedural requirements, see Chapter 7.

If the trust corporation was appointed jointly with another attorney, Sch 3 Pt I para 6 EPAA 1985 applies. This provides that in s 8(4) references to 'the attorney' will be read as including references to any attorney under the power. Thus the mere fact that there is another attorney will not prevent the revocation of a joint power if one attorney is a trust corporation which is insolvent.

If the trust corporation was appointed jointly and severally with another attorney, s 11(7) applies with the effect that the registration will not be cancelled on the winding up or dissolution of the trust corporation if there is one attorney who is still able to act.

Entering into a voluntary arrangement, the making of an administration order or the appointment of a receiver may all have the effect of revoking the power; the EPAA 1985 does not deal specifically with these situations, but it is submitted that any such revocation will take effect as a disclaimer of the power.

Section 5(1) and (2) Powers of Attorney Act 1971 may operate to protect the donee and persons dealing with him.

7. Death

As with ordinary powers, the death of the donor or donee of the power revokes the power, and the court must cancel the registration of an enduring power if it is satisfied that the power has been revoked by the death of the donor or donee of the power (s 8(4)(d) EPAA 1985). The procedure for cancelling the registration is discussed in Chapter 7.

If joint attorneys have been appointed, Sch 3 Pt I para 6 EPAA 1985 provides that in s 8(4) references to 'the attorney' will be read as including references to any attorney under the power. The effect of this is that if one joint attorney has died, the court must confirm the revocation of the power, even though another joint attorney is still alive.

However, if more than one attorney has been appointed, and their authority is joint and several, s 11(7) applies, with the effect that on the death of one attorney the registration remains in force as regards the surviving attorneys.

Section 5(1) and (2) Powers of Attorney Act 1971 may operate to protect the donee and persons dealing with the attorney.

8. Disclaimer of power

The donee of an enduring power can disclaim at any time, but under s 2(12) EPAA 1985 the disclaimer is invalid unless and until the attorney gives notice to the donor.

If the attorney is under a duty to apply for registration under s 4 EPAA 1985, s 4(6) provides that no disclaimer will be valid unless and until the attorney gives notice to the court or the Public Trustee. In the case of joint and several attorneys, this restriction applies only to those attorneys who have reason to believe that the donor is or is becoming mentally incapable (Sch 3 Pt II para 8).

Once the enduring power has been registered, under s 7(1)(b) EPAA 1985 no disclaimer of the power is valid until the attorney gives notice to the court or the Public Trustee. Under s 8(4) the court must cancel the registration of an instrument on receiving notice of disclaimer. If one joint attorney disclaims, the registration must be cancelled completely (Sch 3 Pt I para 6), but if a joint and several attorney disclaims, the registration remains valid as regards the other attorney(s).

Rule 11(7) Court of Protection (Enduring Powers of Attorney) Rules 1994 (SI 1995 No 3047) provides that the disclaimer takes effect on the day on which the notice of disclaimer is received at the Public Trust Office.

9. Mental incapacity

The mental incapacity of the donor of the power will not cause its revocation (s 1(1)(a) EPAA 1985) but, apart from some limited exceptions, the donee cannot do anything under the power until the instrument creating the power is registered (s 1(1)(b) EPAA 1985). The exceptions are contained in s 1(2), and permit the attorney to maintain the donor or prevent loss to his estate, or to maintain himself or other persons in so far as s 3(4) permits him to do so. Section 3(4) provides:

'Subject to any conditions or restrictions contained in the instrument, an attorney under an enduring power, whether general or limited, may (without obtaining any consent) act under the power so as to benefit himself or other persons than the donor to the following extent but no further, that is to say –

(a) he may so act in relation to himself or in relation to any other person if the donor might be expected to provide for his or that person's needs respectively; and

(b) he may do whatever the donor might be expected to do to meet those needs.'

Under s 1(1)(b) the court may direct or authorise the attorney to take action under the power.

Section 2(11) EPAA 1985 provides that an enduring power will be revoked on the exercise by the court of any of its powers under Pt VII Mental Health Act 1983 if, but only if, the court so directs.

The mental incapacity of the donee will revoke the power, and the court must cancel the registration of an enduring power if it is satisfied that it has been so revoked (s 8(4)(d) EPAA 1985).

The procedure for registering and cancelling the registration of an enduring power of attorney is discussed in Chapter 7.

10. Illegality

The EPAA 1985 does not specifically deal with this point; presumably the principles which apply to ordinary powers apply also to enduring powers. If the court is satisfied that, having regard to all the circumstances and in particular the attorney's relationship to or connection with the donor, the attorney is unsuitable to be the donor's attorney, it can cancel the registration (s 8(4)(g) EPAA 1985).

Summary

- The authority of the donee of a power will cease if the power is granted for a limited period and that period has elapsed, or the power is granted for a specific purpose and that purpose is fulfilled.
- A power may be revoked expressly or impliedly.
- The bankruptcy of the donor of a power will revoke the

power; an ordinary power will not necessarily be revoked by the bankruptcy of the donee, but an enduring power will be.

- The winding up or dissolution of a company will usually revoke a power.

- Death of the donor or donee revokes a power.

- A power can be disclaimed, but if it is an enduring power, notice must be given to the donor, or to the court if (a) the attorney is under a duty to register the enduring power or (b) it has already been registered.

- The mental incapacity of the donor or donee will revoke an ordinary power, but the mental incapacity of the donor will not revoke an enduring power.

- Illegality will revoke a power.

- Powers may be irrevocable.

- If it is an enduring power, notice of revocation may have to be given to the court.

Chapter 7

Registration of enduring powers of attorney

The Enduring Powers of Attorney Act 1985 ('EPAA 1985') contains safeguards to protect donors, donees and third parties. The donor of an enduring power is under an obligation to register the power and to give notice to the closest relatives. The provisions of the EPAA 1985 and the regulations dealing with registration and notification must now be examined in detail.

Subsections 11(2) and (3) provide that the EPAA 1985 applies to joint and to joint and several powers (with some modifications which are set out in the text).

1. Duty to register

An enduring power of attorney operates as an ordinary power until the attorney has reason to believe that the donor is or is becoming mentally incapable (s 4(1) EPAA 1985). The attorney is then under a duty to apply to the court as soon as practicable for the registration of the instrument creating the power (s 4(2)).

The duty arises only if the attorney has reason to believe that the donor *is or is becoming* mentally incapable. The donor does not have to be mentally incapable before the duty to register arises; the duty arises as soon as the attorney has reason to believe that the donor is becoming incapable. It is of course often difficult to decide when a donor has become mentally incapable, but the requirement to register as soon as the attorney has reason to believe that the donor is becoming incapable avoids this difficulty.

Section 13(1) provides that 'mentally incapable' or 'mental incapacity' means, in relation to any person, that he is incapable by reason of mental disorder of managing and administering his property and affairs.

What happens if the attorney considers that the donor is or is becoming incapable, but has doubts about the validity of the power, for example if the attorney thinks the donor may not have had capacity to grant the power originally? In an article in *The Law Society's Gazette* (29 April 1987) PD Lewis, Assistant Public Trustee, stated at page 1220 that the Master had decided that in this type of case the attorney would not be in breach of the duty imposed by s 4(2) if he made an application under s 4(5) to have the validity of the power determined (see page 53).

2. Notice to relatives

(a) Who is entitled to notice?

Section 4(3) and Sch 1 EPAA 1985 require the attorney to give notice to various relatives and the donor before making an application for the registration of an enduring power. Under Sch 1 Pt I para 2(1) EPAA 1985 the following persons are entitled to notice:

(a)   the donor's spouse;

(b)   the donor's children;

(c)   the donor's parents;

(d)   the donor's brothers and sisters, whether of the whole or half blood;

(e)   the widow or widower of a child of the donor;

(f)   the donor's grandchildren;

(g)   the children of the donor's brothers and sisters of the whole blood;

(h)   the children of the donor's brothers and sisters of the half blood;

(i)   the donor's uncles and aunts of the whole blood;

(j)   the children of the donor's uncles and aunts of the whole blood.

Paragraph 8(1) states that an illegitimate child is to be treated as if he were the legitimate child of his father or mother.

In *The Law Society's Gazette* (26 November 1986) PD Lewis at page 3568 raises the question of whether the widow or widower of a child should be notified if he or she has remarried. His view is that notification should be given.

This requirement to give notice could be impossible to satisfy. It is limited by paras 2(2), 2(3) and 2(4). Paragraph 2(2) provides that a person is not entitled to receive notice if:

(a)   his name or address is not known to the attorney and cannot be reasonably ascertained by him; or

(b)   the attorney has reason to believe that he has not attained eigh-
       teen years or is mentally incapable (for the definition of
       mental incapacity see s 13(1) EPAA 1985 and page 47).

Paragraphs 2(3) and 2(4) provide that:

(a)   notice does not have to be given to more than three persons;
       but

(b)   if more than one person falls within classes (a) to (j) and at
       least one of those persons is entitled to notice, all the persons
       falling within that class are entitled to notice, unless they are
       not entitled to notice because the conditions of para 2(2) are
       satisfied;

(c)   in determining who is entitled to notice, persons within class
       (a) are to be preferred to those within class (b), persons falling
       within class (b) are to be preferred to those falling within class
       (c); and so on.

It is more than likely that the attorney will be within one of the
classes of person entitled to notice, and to prevent the absurdity of
the attorney having to give notice to himself, para 3(1) provides
that an attorney is not required to give notice to himself or to any
other attorney under the power who is joining in making the application, notwithstanding that he or, as the case may be, the other
attorney is entitled to receive notice by virtue of para 2.

Although the attorney need not give himself notice, he need not
give notice to a more distant person or class on the list in his place
(PD Lewis, *The Law Society's Gazette* (26 November 1986) at page
3567). However, apart from this exception, the requirements of
paras 2(3) and 2(4) must be satisfied.

Paragraph 3(2) authorises the court or the Public Trustee to
dispense with the requirement to give notice if it is satisfied that:

(a)   it would be undesirable or impracticable for the attorney to
       give him notice; or

(b)   no useful purpose would be served by giving him notice.

(b) Form of notice

Rule 7(1) Court of Protection (Enduring Powers of Attorney) Rules
1994 (SI 1994 No 3047) ('CPR') provides that notice must be given
in Form EP1 to those entitled to receive such notice and to any co-
attorney. All such notices must be served within 14 days of each
other. Form EP1 is reproduced in Appendix 3 on page 213. PD
Lewis in *The Law Society's Gazette* (26 November 1986) states at

page 3567 that the form should not be sent out until the enduring power has been executed as the form is drafted on the basis that the power is already in existence.

Rule 7(2) CPR provides that an application to dispense with notice must be made in Form EP3 before any application for registration is made. The procedure on such an application is discussed on pages 59–60.

Section 12 EPAA 1985 empowers the Lord Chancellor to exempt attorneys of such descriptions as he thinks fit from the requirements of the EPAA 1985 to give notice to relatives before registration. No order has yet been made under this provision.

3. Notice to donor

Schedule 1 Pt I para 4(1) EPAA 1985 requires an attorney to give notice to the donor that he intends to apply for registration of the power, but under para 4(2) the court or the Public Trustee may dispense with this requirement if it is satisifed that:

(a) it would be undesirable or impracticable for the attorney to give notice to the donor; or

(b) no useful purpose is likely to be served by giving notice to the donor.

Form EP1 must be used to give notice to the donor, and the application to dispense with notice must be in Form EP3. Under r 16(1) CPR any document required to be given to the donor must be given to him personally, although an agent can be employed to do this (see PD Lewis, *The Law Society's Gazette* (26 November 1986) at page 3567). The procedure on such applications is discussed on pages 59–60.

PD Lewis in *The Law Society's Gazette* (26 November 1986) states at page 3568 that applications to dispense with service on the donor on the ground that he is incapable of understanding the registration procedure are unlikely to succeed, unless there is clear medical evidence that service would be detrimental to the donor's health.

4. Notice to other attorneys

Before making an application for registration, Sch 1 Pt III para 7 EPAA 1985 requires an attorney under a joint and several power to give notice of his intention so to do to any other attorney under the power who is not joining in making the application. Note that if it is a joint power, all the attorneys must apply for registration.

As with the duty to give notice to relatives, an attorney is not entitled to receive notice if:

(a) his address is not known to the applying attorney and cannot reasonably be ascertained by him; or

(b) the applying attorney has reason to believe that he has not attained eighteen years or is mentally incapable (for definition of mental incapacity see s 13(1) EPAA 1985 and page 47).

Under Sch 1 Pt I para 3(2) EPAA 1985, the court or the Public Trustee can dispense with the requirement to give notice if it is satisfied that:

(a) it would be undesirable or impracticable for the attorney to give him notice; or

(b) no useful purpose would be served by giving him notice.

Form EP1 should be used for the notice, and Form EP3 should be used for the application to dispense with the notice.

5. Form and service of notices

Schedule 1 Pt II EPAA 1985 and the Court of Protection (Enduring Powers of Attorney) Rules 1994 (SI 1994 No 3047) ('CPR') prescribe the form of notice to be given to relatives, the donor, and co-attorneys. The Form, EP1, is reproduced on page 213.

Under r 16(1) CPR, the notice must be given to the donor personally.

Schedule 1 Pt IV para 8(2) EPAA 1985 provides that for the purposes of the schedule a notice given by post will be regarded as given on the date on which it was posted. Rule 16(2) CPR provides that the notice will be served on any person other than the donor by sending it by first class post.

Service on a solicitor is also permissible under r 17 CPR unless the solicitor is acting for the donor. The solicitor must endorse on the document or a copy of a statement that he or she accepts the document on behalf of that person, and the document will then be deemed to have been duly sent to that person, and to have been received on the date on which the endorsement was made.

Substituted service is also permissible. Rule 18 provides that where it appears to the court that it is impracticable for any document to be sent in accordance with r 16(2) CPR the court may give such directions for the purpose of bringing the document to the notice of the person to whom it is addressed as it thinks fit.

6. Grounds for objection to registration

A person who is served with notice of an application to apply for registration can object to the registration on various grounds specified in s 6(5) EPAA 1985. The grounds are as follows:

(a) that the power purported to have been created by the instrument was not valid as an enduring power of attorney (for example, that it had not been signed by all or one of the parties);

(b) that the power created by the instrument no longer exists (for example, that it had been revoked);

(c) that the application is premature because the donor is not yet becoming mentally incapable;

(d) that fraud or undue pressure was used to induce the donor to create the power;

(e) that, having regard to all the circumstances and in particular the attorney's relationship to or connection with the donor, the attorney is unsuitable to be the donor's attorney. In the case of joint attorneys, this ground applies to any attorney (Sch 1 Pt I para 4 EPAA 1985).

If it is a joint and several power, objection may be taken to registration on a ground relating to any attorney, or to the power of any attorney whether or not the attorney is an applicant (s 11(5)(c) EPAA 1985).

Under r 10(1) CPR any objections to registrations must be in writing, and must contain:

(a) the name and address of the objector;

(b) the name and address of the donor, if the objector is not the donor;

(c) any relationship of the objector to the donor;

(d) the name and address of the attorney; and

(e) the grounds for objecting to registration of the enduring power.

In *The Law Society's Gazette* (29 April 1987) PD Lewis states at page 1219 that if the objections to registration are not clearly expressed, the objector will be asked to give full particulars, and a copy will be sent to the applicant or his solicitors. A preliminary hearing for directions will be held, and directions may be given for the filing of particulars of the objection, and affidavit evidence, discovery and inspection documents, allocation of a hearing date and costs. It may be that the issues can be resolved in correspondence without the need for a hearing (page 1220). PD Lewis also refers to one case where 'an objector (who had failed to give particulars of his objection after request) was ordered to do so, and to file affidavit evidence in support, with a condition that, in default, his objections should be dismissed. He failed to comply with the order, the objections were dismissed and taxed costs were awarded against him'.

Section 11(6) EPAA 1985 applies to joint and several powers, and provides that the court will not refuse an application for registration if a ground for objection is made out in respect of one attorney, but not as regards another attorney; the court will give effect to it by the prescribed qualification of the registration.

Rule 10(2) CPR provides that any objection to registration received by the court on or after the date of registration will be treated as an application to cancel the registration.

7. Preliminary hearing as to validity of power

An attorney may consider that it is desirable for the court to rule on the validity of a power before applying for registration. Section 4(5) EPAA 1985 permits such an application, and provides that the attorney must comply with any direction given by the court.

8. Leave to bring an application

If a person who has not been served with notice of intention to register an enduring power wants to apply for relief, he must apply to the court or the Public Trustee for leave to do so (r 22 CPR).

9. The application for registration

Rule 8 CPR requires an application for registration of an enduring power to be made in Form EP2, which is reproduced in Appendix 3 on page 214. The form must be lodged with the Public Trust Office.

It is not necessary to file an affidavit of family and property.

The enduring power of attorney must accompany the application; the fee for lodging the application is £50 (r 27 and Sch 2 CPR). Under r 27(3) this fee is payable out of the assets of the donor.

Rule 8 CPR also provides that Form EP2 must be lodged with the Public Trust Office not later than ten days after the date on which:

(a)   notice has been given to the donor and every relative (if any) entitled to receive notice, and every co-attorney; or

(b)   leave has been given to dispense with notice,

whichever may be the later.

Originally the time limit was three days. In *The Law Society's Gazette* (29 April 1987) PD Lewis reports at page 1220 that this time limit is frequently overlooked. Applications to extend the time limit are decided on their merits. He warns that 'it is very important to consider carefully the form of wording of the application to bring out the strength of the application'. Form EP3 should be used for the application for extension of time.

Rule 9(1) CPR provides that application to the court may be by letter unless the court directs that it should be made formally, when Form EP3 must be used; Form EP3 is reproduced in Appendix 3 on page 215.

If the donor appoints two or more persons as joint attorneys, they must all apply for registration. If one joint attorney dies, the survivor(s) cannot exercise the power. If two or more persons are appointed joint and several attorneys, the survivor(s) can continue to exercise the power after the death of one. If the donor appoints successive attorneys, for example an appointment of A, but if he dies, then B, only one attorney should apply for registration. It will be necessary to file affidavit evidence as to which one is entitled to register (PD Lewis, *The Law Society's Gazette* (29 April 1987) at pages 1219 and 1220).

Section 4(7) EPAA 1985 imposes criminal penalties for knowingly making false statements in an application for registration.

If the donor is blind, the attorney or his solicitors will have to inform the court how the donor was notified of the intention to apply for registration (see PD Lewis, *The Law Society's Gazette* (29 April 1987) at page 1220).

There is no need to send to the court copies of Form EP1 served on the donor and relatives (PD Lewis, *The Law Society's Gazette* (26 November 1986) at page 3567). In the same article, the author makes the following points about Form EP2:

- 'The age of the attorney may be shown as "over 18", although the exact age is more informative.'
- 'The date to be given in the third block on the form (the application to register) is the date when the power was executed by the donor ...'

- 'The relevant dates must be included in the fifth and sixth blocks on the form.'

- 'If there are no relatives falling within the class entitled to be notified, it avoids an enquiry from the court if the block is completed to show that, rather than being left blank or crossed through.'

- 'If there is only one attorney, the reference in the sixth block (to notification of co-attorney) should be crossed out.

- 'The final block should be checked to see that it has been signed and dated and that the address where notices should be sent has been inserted.'

- 'Manuscript or typed amendments to the form should be initialled by the attorney(s). Amendments made by the use of correcting fluid are not acceptable; a fresh form should be used.'

- 'Any discrepancy between the spelling of the donor's or attorney's name in the enduring power and in the EP2 should be explained in a covering letter, as should any discrepancy between the donor's address on the EP2 and the address at which (s)he was served.'

10. Effect of application for registration

Section 1(1)(b) EPAA 1985 provides that if the donor becomes mentally incapable, the donee of the power may not do anything under the authority of the power, unless it is permitted under s 1(2), or it is authorised or directed by the court under s 5.

Section 1(2) provides that where an application for registration of a power has been made, the attorney may take action under the power:

(a) 'to maintain the donor or prevent loss to his estate; or

(b) to maintain himself or other persons in so far as section 3(4) permits him to do so'.

Section 11(5)(a) provides that in the case of a joint and several power, an attorney who has not applied for registration may act under s 1(2) as well as an attorney who has applied.

Section 3(4) provides that subject to anything contained in the power, the attorney may act under the power so as to benefit himself or persons other than the donor to the following extent but no further:

(a) he may so act in relation to himself or in relation to any other person if the donor might be expected to provide for his or that person's needs respectively; and

(b) he may do whatever the donor might be expected to do to meet those needs.

11. Simultaneous receipt of application for registration and application to appoint a receiver

PD Lewis in the *The Law Society's Gazette* (29 April 1987) states at page 1219 that if an application for registration of an enduring power of attorney appointing X as attorney is received at the same time as an application to appoint Y as receiver under the Mental Health Act 1983, the court will usually register the power of attorney. If it is not possible to register the power, the court will consider the appointment of a receiver. The reason for this course of action is that it is the course preferred by the donor of the power. The Master may give directions, and may try to resolve the matter through correspondence.

12. Functions of court before registration

Section 5 EPAA 1985 gives the court power to exercise the powers it would have under s 8(2) once the power is registered if the court has reason to believe that the donor may be, or may be becoming, mentally incapable. The power is exercisable whether or not the attorney has made an application for registration; presumably a relative could apply. For a discussion of s 8(2), see pages 62 and 63.

In *The Law Society's Gazette* (29 April 1987) PD Lewis dealt at page 1220 with the situation where an attorney wishes to sell property belonging to the donor before the attorney has applied to register an enduring power, or where there is a pending application for registration. Application must be made under s 5 EPAA 1985, and 'the court must receive evidence giving it reason to believe that the donor may be, or be becoming, mentally incapable and must be satisfied of the need for interim directions. In particular, it will need to be satisfied that, if the house to be sold is the donor's home, there is no reasonable likelihood of the donor returning to live there. If the donor is not yet becoming mentally incapable, the attorney may be able to use the power as an ordinary power, of course without reference to the court'.

The article also suggests that use could be made of s 1(2) (see page 55).

Under Sch 3 Pt I para 3 EPAA 1985, which applies to joint powers, references to 'the attorney' in s 5 are to be read as including references to any attorney under the power. Under s 11(5)(a), which applies to joint and several powers, an attorney who is not an applicant may act under s 5, as well as an attorney who is an applicant, pending the initial determination of the application.

13. Functions of court on application for registration

It should be noted that r 6 CPR authorises the Public Trustee to register an enduring power, or to refuse to register an enduring power on certain grounds. The Public Trustee is also authorised to perform other functions. Section 6 EPAA 1985 provides that if an application for registration has been made in accordance with s 4(3) and (4), the court or the Public Trustee will register the application unless:

(a) it appears to the court or the Public Trustee that there is in force under Pt VII Mental Health Act 1983 an order appointing a receiver for the donor but the power has also not been revoked (s 6(2) EPAA 1985); or

(b) a valid notice of objection to the registration has been received by the court or the Public Trustee before the expiry of five weeks beginning with the date or, as the case may be, the latest date on which the attorneys gave notice to any person under Sch 1; or

(c) it appears from the application that there is no one to whom notice has been given under Sch 1 para 1; or

(d) the court or the Public Trustee has reason to believe that appropriate inquiries might bring to light evidence on which the court could be satisfied that one of the grounds of objection was established (s 6(4)).

If (a) applies, the court or the Public Trustee must refuse the application for registration unless it directs otherwise.

If (b), (c) or (d) apply, the Public Trustee must refer the application to the court (r 6(3) CPR). The court must not make any decision until it has made or caused to be made such inquiries as it thinks appropriate.

Section 6(6) EPAA 1985 provides that in these circumstances if any of the grounds of objection in s 6(5) is established to the satisfaction of the court, the court will refuse the application, but if in such a case it is not so satisfied, the court will register the instrument to which the application relates.

If the court decides that fraud or undue pressure was used to induce the donor to create the power, or that, having regard to all the circumstances and in particular the attorney's relationship to or connection with the donor, the attorney is unsuitable to be the donor's attorney, the court must revoke the power created by the instrument (s 6(7) EPAA 1985).

Rule 6(1) CPR provides that the Public Trustee may refuse to register an enduring power on the ground that:

(a) the power was not in the prescribed form; or

(b) the power was not executed in the prescribed manner by the donor and the attorney; or

(c) the power did not incorporate at the time of execution by the donor the prescribed explanatory information; or

(d) the attorney has not attained eighteen years; or

(e) the attorney is a bankrupt; or

(f) it is a power under s 25 Trustee Act 1925 (power to delegate trusts); or

(g) the power appoints more than one person to be an attorney, and they have not been appointed to act jointly or severally.

If the application for registration is refused, the court may appoint a receiver.

Rule 13(1) CPR provides that if there is no objection to registration, or the objection is withdrawn or dismissed, the enduring power will be registered by the Public Trustee and sealed by the court. The original power stamped with the date of registration is returned to the applicant attorney, but the Public Trustee retains a copy (r 13(2) and 13(5)). Any qualification to the registration imposed by reason of s 11(6) or 11(7) EPAA 1985 must be noted on the register and on the power (r 13(4)). Under r 13(3) any alterations on the face of an instrument when an application for registration is made must be sealed.

Section 6(8) EPAA 1985 provides that when the court refuses an application the instrument must be delivered up to be cancelled, unless the court otherwise directs. But this provision does not apply if the court refuses an application on the ground that it is premature because the donor is not yet becoming mentally incapable.

14. Dispensing with notice of application at the hearing

As described on pages 49 and 51, before applying for registration of the power, it is possible to apply to the court to dispense with service of notice on those people who are required to be served under Sch 1 EPAA 1985. If this is not done, the court or the Public Trustee is empowered under s 6(3) EPAA 1985, at the hearing of the application for registration of the power, to treat the application as if notices have been given if it is satisfied that as regards each such person not served:

(a) it was undesirable or impracticable for the attorney to give him notice; or

(b) no useful prupose is likely to be served by giving him notice.

15. Evidence

Rule 21 CPR authorises the issue of a witness summons in Form EP6.

Under r 19, evidence which has been used in any proceedings relating to the donor may be used at any subsequent stage in those proceedings or in any other proceedings before the court.

16. Hearings

It may be necessary to have a hearing, for example to deal with an objection. Rule 11 CPR applies to the following applications (under EPAA 1985) to the court or, where appropriate, referred to the court by the Public Trustee for relief or for the determination of any question:

- applications to the court for directions or authority under s 1(1)(b);
- applications under s 4(5), prior to an application for registration, for determination of any question as to the validity of the power;
- applications under s 5 for the exercise of any power with respect to the power of attorney or the attorney before registration of the power;
- applications under s 6(3) for directions that notice has been given in accordance with s 4(3);
- applications under s 6(4), which deals with objections and failure to give notice;
- applications under s 8(2) for various matters once the power has been registered;
- applications under s 8(3) for confirmation of the revocation of the power by the donor;

- applications under s 8(4) for cancellation of the registration of a power;
- applications under s 11(5)(c) which deals with objections to registration when more than one attorney is appointed, and not all the attorneys apply for registration;
- applications under Sch 1 para 2(1) which deals with the persons entitled to receive notice of an application for registration of an enduring power;
- applications under Sch 1 para 3(2) to dispense with notice;
- applications under Sch 1 para 4(2) to dispense with notice to donor;
- applications under Sch 1 para 7(1) to dispense with service of notice on other attorneys.

Rule 11 applies only if the application is not made simultaneously with the application for registration of an enduring power.

Rule 9(1) provides that an application may be by letter, unless the court or the Public Trustee directs that the application should be formal, in which case it must be made in Form EP3; this form is reproduced in Appendix 3 on page 215.

Rule 9(2) provides that any application made by letter under r 9(1), other than an objection to registration or disclaimer of attorneyship, must include the name and address of the applicant, the name of the donor if the applicant is not the donor, the form of relief or determination required and the grounds for the application. Rule 11(2) provides that on receipt of an application, the court may decide that no hearing should be held, or it may fix an appointment for directions, or for the application to be heard. Under r 11(3) the court may, on application or of its own motion, give such directions as it thinks proper. Notification of an appointment for directions, or for a hearing must be given by the applicant to the attorney (if he is not the applicant), to any objector, and to any other person directed by the court to be notified (r 11(4)), and the applicant and any person given notice of the appointment or hearing may attend or be represented (r 11(5)). Under r 11(6) the court can of its own motion make such order or give such directions as it thinks fit.

Rule 23 CPR provides that all persons who receive notice under r 11(4) must be notified by the applicant of the court's decision, and must also be sent a copy of any order made or directions given.

17. Notice of hearings

Unless the court directs otherwise, r 15(1) provides that ten clear days' notice must be given in the case of:

- an application to dispense with notice to the donor;
- an application to dispose of the donor's property before registration; and
- an objection to registration of an enduring power,

to the attorney, the donor, every relative as defined in r 3(1) CPR, to any co-attorney and to such other persons who appear to the court to be interested as the court may specify.

Seven clear days' notice must be given of any other application and to any other person interested in the proceeedings (r 15(1)(b)).

The court may extend or abridge these time limits (r 15(3)), and r 15(4) provides that notice of hearing is given if the applicant sends a copy of the application to the person concerned.

18. Consolidation of proceedings

Rule 12 permits the court to consolidate any applications for registration or relief or any objections to registration if it considers that the proceedings relating to them can more conveniently be dealt with together.

19. Effect of registration

Section 7(1) EPAA 1985 provides that the effect of registration of an enduring power is that:

(a) no revocation of the power by the donor will be valid unless and until the court confirms the registration under s 8(3);

(b) no disclaimer of the power will be valid unless and until the attorney gives notice to the court or the Public Trustee;

(c) the donor may not extend or restrict the scope of the authority conferred by the instrument;

(d) no instruction or consent given by the donor after registration will, in the case of consent, confer any right and, in the case of an instruction, impose or confer any obligation or right on, or create any liability of, the attorney or other persons having notice of the instruction or consent. In effect, once the power is registered, the donor cannot give any consent or instructions.

Section 7(2) provides that s 7(1) applies for so long as a power is registered, even though the donor is mentally capable. For a further discussion of s 7, see page 79.

20. Functions of court with regard to registered powers

Section 8 EPAA 1985 gives the court wide powers once a power has been registered. Under subs (2) the court may:

(a) determine any question as to the meaning or effect of the instrument;

(b) give directions with respect to:

   (i) the management or disposal by the attorney of the property and affairs of the donor;

   (ii) the rendering of accounts by the attorney and the production of records kept by him for the purpose;

   (iii) the remuneration or expenses of the attorney, whether or not in default of or in accordance with any provision made by the instrument, including directions for the repayment of excessive, or the payment of additional remuneration;

(c) require the attorney to furnish information or produce documents or things in his possession as attorney;

(d) give any consent or authorisation to act which the attorney would have to obtain from a mentally incapable donor;

(e) authorise the attorney to act so as to benefit himself or other persons than the donor otherwise than in accordance with s 3(4) and (5) (but subject to any conditions or restrictions contained in the instrument);

(f) relieve the attorney wholly or partly from any liability which he has or may have incurred on account of a breach of his duties as attorney.

Under Sch 3 Pt I para 5, which applies to joint attorneys, reference to 'the attorney' under s 8(2) includes references to any attorney under the power.

For a discussion of s 3(4) and (5), see pages 76 to 79.

The rights of an attorney to indemnity and remuneration are discussed in Chapter 10.

The question of the extent of the powers of the court under s 8(2)(b)(i) was discussed in *Re R* [1990] 2 WLR 1219. In that case R appointed her nephew as her attorney under an enduring power of attorney which was registered under the EPAA 1985. The applicant had been employed by R as a cook and housekeeper, but she alleged that she had become a companion, and that R had led her to believe that R would provide for her for the rest of her life. R went into a nursing home, and the applicant remained in R's flat. The attorney gave her notice terminating her employment, and wanted possession of the flat. The applicant asked the court to make provision for her under s 8(2)(b)(i) EPAA 1985. The application was refused. Vinelott J held that the section was concerned with administrative matters, and did not give the court power to dispose of the whole of R's property.

In *The Law Society's Gazette* (29 April 1987) PD Lewis states at page 1220 that the court should be asked to give directions in only the most exceptional circumstances.

21. Assumption of full mental capacity

Section 13(2) EPAA 1985 provides that any question arising under or for the purposes of the EPAA 1985 as to what the donor of the power might at any time be expected to do will be determined by assuming that he had full mental capacity at the time but otherwise by reference to the circumstances existing at that time.

22. Effect of failure to register

The EPAA 1985 does not provide for any penalties for non-registration. However, a donor who acts under an enduring power which should have been registered may be liable to a third party.

23. Cancellation of registration

Section 8(4) EPAA 1985 provides that the court will cancel the registration of an enduring power in the following circumstances:

(a) on confirming the revocation of the power under s 8(3), or on receiving notice of disclaimer under s 7(1)(b);

(b) on giving a direction revoking the power on exercising any of its powers under Pt VII Mental Health Act 1983;

(c) on being satisfied that the donor is and is likely to remain mentally capable;

(d) on being satisfied that the power has expired or has been revoked by the death or bankruptcy of the donor, or the death, mental incapacity or bankruptcy of the attorney or, if the attorney is a body corporate, its winding up or dissolution;

(e)   on being satisfied that the power was not a valid or subsisting enduring power when registration was effected;

(f)   on being satisfied that fraud or undue pressure was used to induce the donor to create the power; or

(g)   on being satisfied that, having regard to all the circumstances and in particular the attorney's relationship to or connection with the donor, the attorney is unsuitable to be the donor's attorney.

The Public Trustee can cancel the registration of an enduring power revoked by the bankruptcy of the attorney (r 6(1)(c)). Notice of disclaimer can also be served on the Public Trustee (r 6(1)(g)). The procedure for cancellation is discussed on pages 59 and 60.

In *The Law Society's Gazette* (29 April 1987) PD Lewis states at page 1220 that if 'an application is made to cancel a registration on the ground that the donor has recovered, the court will expect to see written confirmation from the donor that he agrees, together with confirmation that he is not seeking to revoke the EPA. The original of any medical report or certificate will also need to be shown'.

If it is a joint power, Sch 3 Pt I para 6 EPAA 1985 provides that references to 'the attorney' include references to any attorney under the power, so that if, for example, one joint attorney becomes bankrupt, the registration must be cancelled completely so that the power ceases to have any effect.

Under s 11(7), which applies to joint and several powers, the court must not cancel any registration of an enduring power for any of the causes vitiating registration if there is one attorney who is not affected by those causes; instead the court must qualify the registration. So if one joint and several attorney becomes bankrupt, the registration will remain valid for the other attorney(s).

If the court is satisfied that grounds (f) or (g) exist, it must revoke the power created by the instrument (s 8(5) EPAA 1985); if the registration is cancelled on any ground other than (c), the instrument must be delivered up to be cancelled, unless the court otherwise directs (s 8(6)).

Rule 26(1) CPR provides that if the registration of an enduring power of attorney is cancelled, the court will direct the Public Trustee to cancel the registration of the power, and to send a notice to the attorney requiring him to deliver to the Public Trustee the original instrument. If the instrument has been destroyed, the attorney served with notice under para 1 must give the Public Trustee written details of the date on which the instrument was lost or destroyed and the circumstances in which that occurred (r 26(3)). Under r 26(4) CPR where registration is cancelled on any ground other than (c), the court will direct the Public Trustee to mark the power of attorney as cancelled or, where appropriate, the Public Trustee will do so of his own motion.

24. Reviews and appeals

Rule 24(1) enables a person who is aggrieved by a decision of the court not made on a hearing or a decision of the Public Trustee, within eight days of the date on which the decision was given, to have the decision reviewed by the court. However, no application for review lies from any decision in relation to the exercise of the court's power under r 86 CPR (r 24(2)); r 86 deals with the remission or postponement of the payment of court fees.

On reviewing a decision, the court may confirm or revoke the decision or may make or give any other order or decision.

Rule 25(1) permits any person aggrieved by any order or decision of the court on a hearing to appeal to a judge within fourteen days from the date of entry of the order or, as the case may be, from the date of the decision. Under r 25(2), the appellant must serve notice of appeal in Form EP7 on:

- every person who is directly affected by the decision; and
- any other person whom the court may direct, and

the appellant must lodge a copy at the court office.

The court fixes the time and place at which the appeal is to be heard, and notifies the appellant who must then notify every person who has been served with notice of appeal (r 25(3)). Further evidence can be filed only with leave of the judge (r 25(4)).

25. Time

Rule 5 contains provisions for the computation of time. Rule 5(1) provides that where the time so fixed for doing an act in the court office expires on a day on which the office is closed, and for that reason the act cannot be done on that day, the act will be in time if it is done on the next day on which the office is open.

Rule 5(2) provides that where the act is required to be done within a specified period after or from a specified date, the period starts immediately after that date.

Rule 5(3) provides that where the period in question consists of three days or less and which includes a day on which the court office is closed, that day will be excluded.

26. Privacy of documents filed in court

Rule 20(1) provides that any person who has filed an affidavit or other document is entitled on request, unless the court otherwise directs, to be supplied by the court with a copy of it.

Rule 20(2) permits an attorney or his solicitor to have a search made for, and may inspect and request a copy of, any document filed in proceedings relating to the enduring power of attorney under which the attorney has been appointed.

Apart from these exceptions, no documents filed in the court or Public Trust Office are open to inspection without the leave of the court, and no copy of any such document or extract can be taken by or issued to any person without such leave (r 20(3)).

27. Searches and copies

Rule 14(1) authorises any person to request the Public Trustee to search the register, and to say whether an enduring power of attorney has been registered. Form EP4 must be used for the search, and the appropriate fee must be paid.

Under r 14(2) the court or the Public Trustee may supply any person with an office copy of a registered enduring power if it is satisfied that he has good reason for requesting a copy and that it is not reasonably practicable to obtain a copy from the attorney.

Rule 14(3) provides that an 'office copy' is a photocopy or facsimile of an enduring power of attorney, marked as an office copy and sealed. However the office copy need not contain the explanatory information endorsed on the original power (r 14(4)).

Summary

- As soon as the attorney has reason to believe that the donor is or is becoming mentally incapable, the attorney must apply for registration of the power.
- Before application is made, notice must be given to various relatives.
- Notice must also be given to the donor.

- In certain circumstances the court or the Public Trustee can dispense with the requirements of notice.

- A person served with notice of application can object to registration on various specified grounds.

- The effect of an application for registration is that the attorney cannot do anything under the power, although there are some limited exceptions to this rule.

- Once the power is registered, the attorney can continue to act.

- The registration can be cancelled on various grounds.

Chapter 8

Extent of the authority

An attorney is under no duty to exercise the power, unless there is some contractual obligation to do so. For example, if a solicitor or accountant in private practice is appointed by a client to be his attorney, there may be a binding contract under which the solicitor or accountant is under a duty to exercise the power; if there is no such contractual relationship, the attorney need not exercise the power, although usually he or she will want to do so because, for example, the donor is a relative.

If the donor is prepared to exercise the power, the extent of the authority will depend on the express terms of the power, but in some situations the law imposes limitations on this power. There is considerable overlap between the powers of an attorney under an ordinary and an enduring power, but because there are differences it is necessary to consider each power separately.

I. Ordinary powers of attorney

1. Actual authority

An attorney can do anything within the actual authority conferred by the power. This authority may permit the attorney to do anything which the donor of the power could have lawfully done, or it may be limited to a particular transaction, for example the sale of a particular house. The interpretation of a limited power of attorney is discussed on pages 69 to 72.

If a general power is to be granted, use should be made of the general power of attorney form set out in Sch 1 Powers of Attorney Act 1971 (the form is reproduced in Appendix 3 on page 209). Section 10(1) Powers of Attorney Act 1971 provides that a general power of attorney in that form, or in a form to the like effect but expressed to be made under the Act, operates to confer:

(a) on the donee of the power; or

(b) if there is more than one donee, on the donees acting jointly or acting jointly and severally, as the case may be,

authority to do on behalf of the donor anything which he can lawfully do by an attorney.

This is a very wide power which, for example, permits the attorney to operate the donor's bank or building society account, sell the donor's house or flat, buy a house or flat, sell and buy stocks and shares and even run a business.

However, subs (2) provides that the attorney cannot exercise functions which a donor has as a trustee or personal representative or as a tenant for life or statutory owner within the meaning of the Settled Land Act 1925. Trustees wishing to delegate may make use of other statutory provisions. Under s 25 Trustee Act 1925, a trustee can delegate by power of attorney, and for a maximum period of twelve months, the trusts, powers and discretions vested in him; and under s 9 Trusts of Land and Appointment of Trustees Act 1996 a trustee of land may delegate his functions by power of attorney to any beneficiary (both these sections are discussed further in Chapter 9).

A further limitation on the power in s 10(1) is illustrated by *Clauss v Pir* [1987] 2 All ER 752. In that case, the defendant was required by a court order to file an affidavit verifying a list of documents. The affidavit was sworn by his wife to whom he had granted a power of attorney. It was held 'that a party cannot do by an attorney some act the competency to do which arises by virtue of some duty of a personal nature requiring skill or discretion for its exercise' (page 755). The argument that s 7, which deals with the execution of instruments by the donee of a power of attorney, permitted this was rejected on the ground that the section was merely procedural, and did not enlarge the authority of the donee (page 756). For a discussion of s 7, see page 115.

If the attorney is authorised to begin court proceedings, they should be in the name of the donor (*Jones and Saldhana v Gurney* [1913] WN 72).

2. Interpretation of a limited power

(a) Limited powers

If a limited power is to be granted, great care must be exercised in drafting the power to ensure that the attorney is authorised to carry out the contemplated transaction, as the courts construe powers of attorney very strictly. In *Bryant, Powis and Bryant Ltd v La Banque du Peuple* [1893] AC 170 Lord Macnaghten said at page 177:

'Nor was it disputed that powers of attorney are to be construed strictly – that is to say, that where an act purporting to be done under a power of attorney is challenged as being in excess of the authority conferred by the power, it is necessary to show that on a fair construction of the whole instrument the authority in question is to be found within the four corners of the instrument, either in express terms or by necessary implication.'

In *Re Dowson and Jenkins's Contract* [1904] 2 Ch 219 a transferee of a mortgage had entered into possession of the mortgaged property, and executed a power of attorney. This power authorised the attorney 'to sell any real or personal property now or hereafter belonging to me by public auction or by private contract, and subject to any condition as to title or otherwise'. The attorney sold the property, but it was held that the power of attorney did not authorise him to do this. The power did not authorise the sale of property mortgaged to the donor.

However, in *Hawksley v Outram* [1892] 3 Ch 359 a partner granted another partner a power of attorney authorising the attorney 'to sell, or concur in selling, any of my real, leasehold, or personal property to any person or persons, company or companies whatsoever, and either by public auction or privately, upon such terms, subject to such special or other conditions, and in such manner as the attorney shall approve ...'. The attorney joined in a sale of the partnership business, and agreed that the vendors would not carry on business within fifty miles of a certain place. The Court of Appeal was of the opinion that the restraint of trade was authorised by the power of attorney.

(b) Limited power followed by a general power

If there is a limited power followed by a general power, the general power will be construed as restricted to the purposes permitted by the limited power. In *Perry v Holl* (1860) 2 De G F & J 38, 45 ER 536 Lord Campbell LC at page 48, 540 said:

'I fully agree with the cases cited by Mr Craig to show that, if there is a power of attorney to do a particular act followed by general words, these general words are not to be extended beyond what is necessary for doing that particular act for which the power of attorney is given.'

An example of the application of this rule is *Lewis v Ramsdale* (1886) 55 LT 179. According to the headnote to the case, A gave a power of attorney to B to manage real estate, recover debts, settle actions, also to 'sell and convert into money' personal property and to execute and perform any contract, agreement, deed, writing or thing that might in B's opinion be necessary or proper for effectuating the purpose aforesaid, or any of them, and 'for all or any of these purposes' of those presents to use A's name and generally to do any other act whatsoever which in B's opinion ought to be done in or about A's concerns as fully as if A were present and did the same, his desire being that all matters respecting the same should be under the full management of B. It was held that the general words were limited by the special purpose of the power of attorney, and did not authorise a mortgage of personal property.

(c) Effect of recitals

Care must also be taken if the power contains recitals, for example a statement of the reasons for the granting of power. In *Rooke v Lord Kensington* (1856) 2 K & J 753, 69 ER 986 Sir W Page Wood V-C at page 769, 992 stated:

> 'It is true that the courts have held ... that you cannot control clear words of a conveyance by words of recital. ... But the expression "clear words of conveyance" is subject to interpretation ... general words are not within that description of clear words of conveyance which cannot be controlled by that recital.'

If the power is limited, the recital will not control it, but if it is a general power, the recital will control it. An example of the operation of this rule is *Danby v Coutts & Co* (1885) 29 Ch D 500 where a wide power of attorney recited that the donor was going abroad, and that he was desirous of appointing attorneys to act for him whilst he was absent from England. It was held that the recital controlled the operative part of the deed, and that the attorney could act only when the donor was abroad.

(d) Wide powers

Even a wide power may not permit some transactions. In *Reckitt v Barnett, Pembroke and Slater Ltd* [1929] AC 176 Sir Harold Reckitt appointed a solicitor as his attorney. The power authorised the solicitor 'to manage his affairs while he was abroad and for the purposes of his affairs to sign and execute all documents which might be necessary or such as the solicitor might think fit'. Later, Sir Harold signed a letter stating that he wished the power to cover the drawing of cheques upon a bank without any restriction. The solicitor issued a cheque in settlement of a private debt in favour of Barrett, Pembroke and Slater Ltd. It was held that the company had to refund the money.

3. Incidental or implied powers

The courts will imply into a power of attorney whatever powers are necessary to carry out the main purpose or purposes of the power. In *Ex parte Wallace; In re Wallace* (1884) 14 QBD 22 a power of attorney authorised the donee 'to commence and carry on, or to defend at law or in equity, all actions, suits, or other proceedings touching anything in which I or my ships or other personal estate may be in anywise concerned'. It was held that the attorney had power to sign a bankruptcy petition on behalf of the donor. At page 24 Bagallay LJ said:

'No doubt we shall be going a step further in holding that the power authorises the signature of a document on behalf of the principal, but the signature is essential to the doing of the act – the commencement of proceedings in bankruptcy – which is authorised.'

In *Henley v Soper* (1828) 8 B & C 16, 108 ER 949, a partner gave his son a power of attorney 'to act on his behalf in dissolving a partnership, with authority to appoint any other person as he might see fit'. The son submitted the accounts to arbitration, and it was held that he had power to do so.

In *Ex parte Frampton; In the Matter of Frampton* (1859) 1 De G & F & J 263 the appellant left the country, but appointed his uncle Edward Frampton his general agent for settling such of his affairs as remained to be settled. He was adjudicated bankrupt, and Edward Frampton instructed solicitors to dispute the adjudication. It was held that Edward had power to instruct solicitors to do this.

However it is very unwise for an attorney to rely on incidental or implied powers except in clear cases as the courts will not carry this idea too far. In *Harper v Godsell* (1870) LR 5 QB 422 Porro, a partner in B Williams & Co, gave Newton, one of his partners, a power of attorney in the following terms:

'for the purposes hereinafter expressed, that is to say, for the purposes of exercising for me, all or any of the powers and priv- ileges conferred by a certain indenture of partnership constituting the firm B Williams & Co ... and to receive and give receipts for all sums of money payable to me by virtue of the said indenture and all other debts or sums of money or securities for money which may be at any time due or payable to me in the United Kingdom and generally to do, execute, and perform any other act, deed, matter or thing whatsoever which ought to be done, executed, or performed, in or about my concerns, engagements, and business of every nature and kind to all intents and purposes as I myself could do if I were present and did the same in my own proper person, it being my intent and desire that all matters and things respecting the same shall be under the full management and direction of my said attorney'.

Newton executed deeds dissolving the partnership, and assigning Porro's share. It was held that these actions were not authorised by the power. Mellor J said at page 429:

'... I think it is clear that the power of attorney refers only to things done in furtherance of partnership purposes, and that it does not extend to give a power to dissolve the partnership.'

It was also held that the general words of the power did not have an unrestricted effect because they were cut down by the special terms of the first part of the power.

In *Jacobs v Morris* [1902] 1 Ch 816 the plaintiff was a tobacco merchant, and he was authorised 'to purchase and to make and enter into, sign and execute any contract or agreement with any persons, firm, company or companies for the purchase of any goods or merchandise in connection with the business carried on by me ...'. The attorney purported to act under the power of attorney, and obtained a loan from a firm of cigar merchants. The merchants did not read the power. It was held that the power of attorney did not confer any implied authority to borrow.

Great care must thus be taken when drafting a limited power to ensure that the attorney is given the powers that he or she will need. A power to sell a property might not authorise the mortgaging or leasing of the property, and it is possible that it might not permit the attorney to take proceedings against a purchaser for breach of contract.

4. Gifts and wills

Unless specifically authorised, an attorney has no power to make gifts (*Re Bowles* (1874) 31 LT 365).

An attorney cannot make a will for the donor. This topic is examined in more detail in Chapter 15.

5. Ratification

An unauthorised act by the donee of a power can be ratified subsequently by the donor of the power. According to Wright J in *Firth v Staines* [1897] 2 QB 70 at page 75, to constitute a valid ratification three conditions must be satisfied:

- the agent whose act is sought to be ratified must have purported to act for the principal;
- at the time the act was done the agent must have had a competent principal;
- at the time of ratification the principal must be legally capable of doing the act himself.

Thus there will be no ratification if the donee purports to act for himself, or at the time when the act was done, or the time of ratification, the principal was mentally incapacitated.

In *Imperial Bank of Canada v Begley* [1936] 2 All ER 367, a Privy Council case, the respondent executed a power of attorney which conferred a very wide power on the donee. The donee transferred money from the respondent's account to his own account at the appellant bank. Subsequently the respondent took a promissory note from the donee for the amount transferred. It was held that the respondent had not ratified the transfer as the donee was not acting as agent for the respondent but for himself. At page 374 it was said:

> 'The first essential to the doctrine of ratification, with its necessary consequence of relating back, is that the agent shall not be acting for himself, but shall be intending to bind a named or ascertainable principal.'

An attorney may be appointed by a company which has not been formed. Section 36C Companies Act 1985, which came into force on 31 July 1990, provides that a contract which purports to be made by or on behalf of the company at a time when the company has not been formed has effect as one made with the person purporting to act for the company or as agent for it, and he is personally liable on the contract accordingly.

6. Execution of documents

Section 7(1) Powers of Attorney Act 1971, as amended by the Law of Property (Miscellaneous Provisions) Act 1989, provides that the donee of a power of attorney may, if he thinks fit:

(a) execute any instrument with his own signature; and

(b)   do any other thing in his own name,

by the authority of the donor of the power; and any doc ment executed or thing done in this manner is as effective as if exe cuted or done by the donee with the signature and seal, or, as the case may be, in the name, of the donor of the power.

Thus an attorney can execute a document either in the name of the donor or in his own name.

If a company has appointed a person as attorney to convey any interest in property in the name or on behalf of the company, the attorney may execute the conveyance by signing the name of the corporation in the presence of at least one witness (s 74(3) Law of Property Act 1925). Section 7(2) Powers of Attorney Act 1971, as amended by the Law of Property (Miscellaneous Provisions) Act 1989, provides that for the avoidance of doubt an instrument to which s 74(3) Law of Property Act 1925 applies may be executed either as provided in that subsection or as provided in s 7 Powers of Attorney Act 1971.

If a company is appointed an attorney, s 74(4) Law of Property Act 1925 provides that an officer appointed for that purpose by the board of directors may execute the deed or other instrument in the name of such other person.

7. Delegation

The basic rule is that an agent has no right to delegate – *delegatus non potest delegare*. But having decided on a course of action authorised by the power, an attorney has authority to employ, if necessary, solicitors, estate agents, accountants, builders, plumbers and so on to implement that decision (*Ex parte Frampton; In the Matter of Frampton* (1859) 1 De G & F & J 263, CA). For example, an attorney authorised to sell a property cannot delegate the decision as to whether to sell, or as to whether a particular offer should be accepted. But having decided to sell, the attorney can instruct an estate agent to find a buyer, and a solicitor to deal with the conveyancing.

It is common for brokers to be given a discretion as to the management of stocks and shares. In addition, the introduction of CREST means that shares may be held by a nominee. If the donor has shareholdings, it may be desirable to give the donee of any power the power to entrust a broker with management of shares, and to hold them in the names of nominees.

II. Enduring powers of attorney

It will be recalled that the donee of an enduring power is under a duty to apply for registration of the power if he has reason to believe that the donor is, or is becoming, mentally incapable. Registration does not alter the extent of the attorney's authority, and so third parties dealing with an attorney under an enduring power which has been registered should still have a look at the power to ensure that the transaction is authorised by it. For a discussion of the donee's powers between the application for registration and registration, see pages 55–60.

1. Actual authority

As with ordinary powers, enduring power may confer a general or limited authority on the donee. Section 3(1) EPAA 1985 provides that an enduring power may confer general authority on the attorney to act on the donor's behalf in relation to all or a specified part of the property and affairs of the donor and may confer on him authority to do specified things on the donor's behalf, and the authority may, in either case, be conferred subject to conditions and restrictions. The prescribed form has provision for a general or limited power.

Although s 3(1) permits limited powers, or powers subject to restrictions or conditions, it may be undesirable to grant a limited power. A limited power may not authorise all the transactions which might be desirable (see the Law Commission's Report on *The Incapacitated Principal* (Law Com No 122 Cmnd 8977 at page 30).

If a general power is granted, s 3(2) EPAA 1985 provides that where an instrument is expressed to confer general authority on the attorney, it operates to confer, subject to restrictions on gifts and to any conditions or restrictions contained in the instrument, authority to do on behalf of the donor anything which the donor can lawfully do by an attorney. Thus a donee under a general power can, for example, sell or mortgage the donor's house, operate bank and building society accounts, and buy and sell shares.

Section 3(4) permits an attorney under a general or limited enduring power to benefit himself or persons other than the donor, but there are limits to this power. The donee can benefit himself or any other person only if the donor of the power might be expected to provide for the donee's or that other person's needs, and he can only do whatever the donor might be expected to do to meet those needs. Thus, if the donor appoints his or her spouse as attorney, the spouse can exercise the power so as to benefit himself or herself, but only if the donor would have done so, and only to the extent to which the donor might be expected to meet those needs. Presumably this power would permit the purchase of expensive luxury items if the conditions in the subsection are satisfied.

The power to make gifts is examined in detail later.

Section 7(1)(c) EPAA 1985 provides that if an enduring power is registered, the donor may not extend or restrict the scope of the authority conferred by the instrument and no instruction or consent given by him after registration will, in the case of an instruction, impose or confer any obligation or right on, or create any liability of, the attorney or other persons having notice of the instruction or consent. Section 7 is discussed on pages 61–62.

2. Interpretation of a limited enduring power

The rules for the interpretation of limited enduring powers are the same as for ordinary powers, and they will be construed strictly.

3. Incidental or implied powers

The rules are the same for enduring powers; however, s 3(4) EPAA 1985 (see above) gives the attorney under an enduring power the power to benefit himself and other persons, subject to any conditions and restrictions contained in the instrument. Thus an enduring power limited to the sale of a house does not authorise gifts.

In addition, s 3(3) EPAA 1985 provides that subject to any conditions or restrictions contained in the instrument, an attorney under an enduring power, whether general or limited, may (without obtaining any consent) execute or exercise all or any of the trusts, powers or discretions vested in the donor as trustee and may (without the concurrence of any person) give a valid receipt for capital or other money paid.

The powers of trustees to appoint attorneys are discussed in Chapter 9.

4. Gifts

An attorney under an ordinary power has no power to make gifts, but s 3(5) EPAA 1985 authorises an attorney to make gifts in certain circumstances. It provides that, subject to any conditions or restrictions contained in the instrument, an attorney under an enduring power, whether general or limited, may (without obtaining any consent) dispose of the property of the donor by way of gift to the following extent but no further:

(a) he may make gifts of a seasonal nature or at a time, or on an anniversary, of a birth or marriage, to persons (including himself) who are related or connected with the donor, and

(b) he may make gifts to any charity to whom the donor made or might be expected to make gifts,

provided that the value of each such gift is not unreasonable having regard to all the circumstances and in particular the size of the donor's estate. This power is without prejudice to the power conferred by s 3(4).

There is no definition of 'related' or 'connected' in the EPAA 1985. In many cases, it will be clear that the person to be benefitted is related or connected, but there could be problems in deciding if an acquaintance is connected with the donor. With charities, the attorney can clearly benefit a charity which the donor has supported in the past, but it might be difficult to justify a gift to a charity which the donor has never supported. However, it would probably be in order to benefit, say, a charity for the relief of cancer if a relative or friend of the donor had died from that disease, even though the donor had not contributed to such a charity in the past.

The value of any gift must not be unreasonable having regard to the circumstances and the size of the estate. Gifts of £5, £10, or £20 are probably in order, unless the estate is very small. A gift of £1,000 out of an estate in excess of £500,000 is clearly permissible, but if the estate is under £10,000, it is probably unreasonable. A gift to a close relative with whom the donor has had no contact for many years is also probably unreasonable.

The court has no power to order the attorney to make gifts. Reference has already been made (page 62) to *Re R* [1990] 2 WLR 1219, where the applicant was employed by R as a cook and housekeeper and lived in R's flat. R gave her nephew an enduring power of attorney, and shortly afterwards she moved to a nursing home. The enduring power of attorney was registered, and the nephew terminated the employment of the applicant, and required her to give up possession of the flat. The applicant alleged that R had promised to provide for her for the rest of her life, and that she had worked for less than the market rate for her services. She applied for provision from R's estate. The application was unsuccessful. Vinelott J said at pages 1222 and 1223:

'It is quite plain, and it is not in dispute, that the only authority that the Court of Protection could have to give directions to the attorney, requiring him to make provision for the applicant, would have to be found, if at all, in s 8(2)(b)(i). The case put by the applicant's counsel is that that subparagraph does give the court unrestricted power to direct an attorney to dispose of any part of the property of the donor by way of gift or in recognition of some moral obligation, unaccompanied by any legal obligation.

I find that an impossible view. Of course the word "disposal" is, in some contexts, capable of being given a very wide meaning, and could include a disposition by way of gift. But it seems to me that in the context of section 8 it cannot have been intended that it should bear that wide meaning. It is in a paragraph, (b), which is plainly concerned with administrative matters: the management of the donor's property; the rendering of accounts and the determination of the remuneration of the attorney. These are all part of the jurisdiction which the court is given to supervise the conduct of the attorney and to see that he is exercising his powers of management and administration properly. It would be remarkable, in a paragraph directed to matters of that sort, to find an unrestricted power given to the court to dispose of the whole of the donor's property by way of gift ...'.

An attorney cannot make a will on behalf of the donor of the power; this topic is examined in more detail in Chapter 15.

5. Ratification

The rules are the same as for ordinary powers until the power has been registered, but if the power is registered, and the donee enters into a transaction not permitted by the enduring power, the donor cannot ratify that transaction. This is because s 7(1)(c) EPAA 1985 provides that no consent given after registration can confer any right. However, where a power is registered s 8(2)(d) EPAA 1985 authorises the court to give any consent or authorisation to act which the attorney would have to obtain from a mentally capable donor. On the face of it, this is wide enough to permit the court to ratify an act outside the authority conferred by an enduring power, but in the light of *Re R* it seems unlikely that the court would adopt such a construction.

Section 8(2)(f) permits the court to relieve the attorney wholly or partly from any liability which he has or may have incurred on account of a breach of his duties as attorney. Perhaps this subsection could be used to ratify an act outside the authority of the attorney.

6. Execution of documents

There is nothing in the EPAA 1985 dealing with the execution of documents, and so the same rules apply to both ordinary and enduring powers.

7. Delegation

There is no specific provision dealing with delegation in the EPAA 1985, and so the rule is the same as for ordinary powers; delegation is not permissible, although the attorney may employ others to carry out his or her decisions.

III. Powers with a foreign element

If a power is entered into abroad, and it is intended that it should be used in England and Wales, it will be governed by English law. In *Sinfra Atkiengesellschaft v Sinfra Ltd* [1939] 2 All ER 675 Lewis J said at page 682:

> 'It is a one-sided instrument ..., and, although it was argued that a different law should be applied to the document depending upon whether the court was considering the formation, the extent, the operation or the termination of the power, I am satisfied that the proper law for an English court to apply is the law of the country in which the power is to operate – that is to say, English law.'

The Contracts (Applicable Law) Act 1990 gives the force of law to various conventions concerning which law governs a contract where there is a choice. The Act applies if there is a contract between the donor and the donee, but the question of whether an agent is able to bind a principal is specifically excluded (Sch 1 Article 1 part 2(f)).

Summary

- An attorney can do anything which he is permitted to do under the power, provided the action is permitted under the general law.

- A limited power will be construed strictly.

- The courts will imply into a limited power whatever incidental powers are necessary to carry out the main purpose of the power.

- An attorney under an enduring power can make gifts; an attorney under an ordinary power cannot do so unless specifically authorised to make them.

- A donor may be able to ratify an unauthorised act, except in the case of an enduring power which has been registered.

- An attorney can execute a document with his own signature, or in the name of the donor.

- An attorney cannot delegate, but he may be able to employ others to carry out the decisions made by the attorney.

Chapter 9

Capacity of donor and donee

This chapter deals with the capacity of the donor or donee to grant a power of attorney and to accept it, and with other related matters which might affect the validity of a power of attorney; it is not concerned with what happens if the donor and donee had capacity to grant and accept the power, but one or both subsequently become incapable. The effect of subsequent incapacity was dealt with in Chapter 6.

The rules for determining whether a donor has capacity at the time when the power is granted are in some cases the same for both ordinary and enduring powers, but there are differences, and so they will be treated separately.

I. Capacity of donor to grant an ordinary power

The rules for determining whether a donor has the capacity to grant a power of attorney are similar to those for determining whether a person has capacity to enter into a contract.

1. Minors

There is some doubt about whether an infant can grant a power of attorney (see page 39 of *Law of Agency* (Sweet & Maxwell, 16th edition, 1996) by Bowstead and Reynolds).

It is submitted that there is no reason why an infant should not confer a revocable authority on an agent, and that the contracts entered into by the agent should bind the infant if they would have done so if the infant had entered into them personally. This was the view of the Law Commission in its Report on *The Incapacitated Principal* (Law Com No 122 Cmnd 8977 at page

3). However, there is a risk that the agent might be personally liable for breach of warranty of authority if the contract does not bind the infant.

2. Mentally disordered persons

A person suffering from mental disorder may not be able to grant a power of attorney. What type of disorder will prevent a person granting a power of attorney? In *Elliot v Ince* (1857) 7 De GM & G 475, 44 ER 186, Lord Cranworth, when dealing with the validity of powers of attorney, said at pages 489, 191:

'... whether at the time when they were executed and acted on respectively [the donor] was of sound mind, so as to be sufficient for the government of herself, her lands and possessions'.

It follows from this quotation that a person suffering from mental disorder can grant a power of attorney in a lucid interval; otherwise the power will be void (see pages 97 to 98). However, in *Law of Agency* by Bowstead and Reynolds it is suggested at page 40 that a person suffering from mental disorder, whose affairs are under the supervision of the Court of Protection under the Mental Health Act 1983, cannot grant a valid power of attorney during a lucid interval. The authority for this assertion is the case of *Re Walker* [1905] 1 Ch 160, where the illegitimate daughter of Benjamin Walker was found to be a lunatic. She suffered from delusions but, at the time she executed a deed poll, she fully understood what was happening and was not suffering from any insane delusions. Vaughan Williams LJ said at page 173:

'I do not think I need say much more with respect to the present application than we ought not to recognise this deed in any way. The Court ought to treat this deed as entirely void, on the plain and simple ground that its execution is inconsistent with the control which the Crown has the right and duty of exercising over the property of a lunatic, and that is a sufficient reason for the conclusion at which we have arrived.'

If there is any doubt about the capacity of a person to grant a power of attorney, his or her doctor should be asked to confirm that the person is capable of managing his or her own affairs. However, there is no mandatory requirement that this should be done.

Even though a power may have been validly granted, an ordinary power will be revoked by the subsequent mental incapacity of the donor. An enduring power will not be so revoked, but the donee of the power is under a duty to register it as soon as he has reason to believe that the donor is or is becoming mentally incapable (s 4(1) EPAA 1985; see Chapter 7).

3. Trustees

Section 10(1) Powers of Attorney Act 1971 provides for a general power of attorney in a specified form, but a trustee cannot use this general power to delegate his powers and discretions as s 10(2) specifically states that the section does not apply to functions which the donor has as a trustee or personal representative or as tenant for life or statutory owner within the meaning of the Settled Land Act 1925.

Section 23(1) and (3) Trustee Act 1925 permit trustees to delegate certain acts to agents, but not the exercise of discretions. Section 23(2) is wider, and permits trustees or personal representatives to appoint any person to act as their agent or attorney for the purpose of selling, converting, collecting, getting in, and executing and perfecting insurances of, or managing or cultivating, or otherwise administering any property, real or personal, movable or immovable, subject to the trust or forming part of the testate's or intestate's estate, in any place outside the United Kingdom. Section 23(2) also permits trustees or personal representatives to appoint any person to act as their agent or attorney for the purpose of executing or exercising any discretion or trust or power vested in them in relation to any such property, with such ancillary powers, and with and subject to such provisions and restrictions as they may think fit, including a power to appoint substitutes. By reason only of their having made such an appointment, the trustees or personal representatives are not responsible for any loss arising thereby.

Thus trustees or personal representatives can delegate the exercise of discretions in addition to administrative acts in relation to property outside the United Kingdom (for a discussion of these provisions see *Law Relating to Trustees* (Butterworth, 15th edition, 1995) by Underhill and Hayton at pages 618–633).

Section 25 Trustee Act 1925, as amended by s 9 Powers of Attorney Act 1971, permits a trustee to delegate his powers and discretions.

Section 25(1) provides that a trustee may, by power of attorney, delegate for a period not exceeding twelve months the execution or exercise of all or any of the trusts, powers and discretions vested in him as trustee either alone or jointly with any other person or persons. Note that the delegation can last only for twelve months, and that a sole trustee as well as a joint trustee can delegate.

Under s 25(2) delegation can be to a trust corporation, but not to the only other trustee, unless that other trustee is a trust corporation.

Section 25(3) requires any instrument creating a power of attorney under the section to be attested by at least one witness.

Section 25(4) states that the donor of a power of attorney under the section must before, or within seven days after, giving the power give written notice to:

(a) each person (other than himself), if any, who under any instrument creating the trust has power (whether alone or jointly) to appoint a new trustee; and

(b) each of the other trustees, if any.

The written notice must contain the following information:

● the date on which the power comes into operation;

● its duration;

● the name of the donee of the power;

● the reason why the power is given;

● where only some are delegated, the trusts, powers and discretions actually delegated.

Failure to comply with these provisions as to notice does not, in favour of a person dealing with the donee of the power, invalidate any act or instrument executed by the donee.

Section 25(5) provides that the donor of a power under the section is liable for the acts or defaults of the donee in the same manner as if they were the acts or defaults of the donor. Any trustee delegating his powers should therefore take care to ensure that the donee is a person who will carry out the trust strictly in accordance with the law.

Section 25(6) provides that for the purpose of executing or exercising the trusts or powers delegated to him, the donee may exercise any of the powers conferred on the donor as trustee by statute or the instrument creating the trust, including the power, for the purpose of the transfer of any inscribed stock, himself to delegate to an attorney power to transfer, but not including the power of delegation conferred by this section. A donee under this section thus stands in the shoes of the trustee, and can even delegate to another attorney the power to transfer inscribed stock.

Section 82(1) Charities Act 1993 permits charity trustees to confer on not less than two of their body a general or limited authority to execute in the names and on behalf of the trustees assurances or other deeds and/or instruments for giving effect to transactions to which the trustees are a party. Under s 82(2) the authority can be conferred in writing or by resolution of a meeting of the trustees.

It may be that trustees can delegate by means of an enduring power; this is discussed on pages 95 to 96.

Section 9 Trusts of Land and Appointment of Trustees Act 1996 has extended the powers of trustees to delegate, although it is a limited power.

Section 9(1) provides that trustees of land can delegate any of their functions by power of attorney. The attorney must be a beneficiary of full age, and must also be entitled to an interest in possession in land subject to the trust. The power must be given by all the trustees jointly, and may be revoked by one or more of them, unless expressed to be irrevocable and to be given by way of security. If another person is appointed trustee, the power is revoked, although the death of any of the original appointors will not cause a revocation. Similarly, if an appointor ceases to be a trustee for any reason, the power will not be revoked (s 9(3)).

The delegation can be for any period or can be indefinite (s 9(5)), but an enduring power cannot be used (s 9(6)) for the purposes of delegation of their functions under s 9(1).

Section 9(4) provides that if the attorney ceases to be a person beneficially entitled to an interest in possession in land, and is the sole attorney, the power is revoked. If there is more than one attorney, the power is still exercisable by the other beneficiaries, provided that the functions delegated to them are specified to be exercised by them jointly and not separately, and they continue to be beneficially entitled to an interest in possession in the land in question.

Section 9(7) provides that the beneficiaries to whom functions have been delegated under s 9(1) are in the same position as trustees with the same duties and liabilities. However, they are not regarded as trustees for any other purpose, including in particular any enactment permitting the delegation of functions by trustees or imposing requirements relating to the payment of capital money.

Section 9(8) deals with the liability of the trustees for the acts and defaults of the attorneys. The trustees are only liable if they did not exercise reasonable care in deciding to delegate the function to the beneficiary or beneficiaries.

Section 9(2) provides protection for persons dealing with the attorney. It provides that if a person deals with the attorney in good faith, the attorney shall be presumed to have been a person to whom the functions could be delegated unless that other person has knowledge at the time of the transaction that he was not such a person.

Purchasers of land from the attorney are also protected if they make a statutory declaration before or within three months after completion of the purchase that they dealt in good faith and did not know that the attorney was a person to whom the functions could not be delegated.

The section applies to trusts where a beneficiary has a life interest, and also to co-ownership where the trustees and beneficiaries are different persons. In the great majority of co-ownership situations the beneficiaries and trustees will be the same persons.

4. Joint tenants or tenants in common

Trustees holding land on trust for joint tenants or tenants in common cannot make use of the general power of attorney contained in s 10 Powers of Attorney Act 1971. They must make use of the limited power contained in s 25 Trustee Act 1925 (*Walia v Michael Naughton Ltd* [1985] 1 WLR 1115). It should be noted that the donee must not be the only other trustee, unless the donee is a trust corporation. This point is particularly important when dealing with jointly owned properties, and in particular when dealing with the matrimonial home, where the legal estate will frequently be vested in spouses on trust for sale for themselves as joint tenants or tenants in common. In this situation, one spouse cannot appoint the other spouse to act as attorney under s 25.

If all the trustees want to grant powers of attorney, there is nothing in the Trustee Act to prevent the appointment of the same person, but if there are only two trustees they cannot appoint each other.

It may be that joint tenants and tenants in common holding on trust for themselves can delegate using an enduring power; this is discussed on page 96.

5. Personal representatives, tenants for life and statutory owners

Tenants for life and statutory owners occur when land is subject to a settlement within the Settled Land Act 1925; these are not very common, and it is no longer possible to create one since the Trusts of Land and Appointment of Trustees Act 1996 came into force on 1 January 1997.

Section 25(8) Trustee Act 1925 permits personal representatives, tenants for life and statutory owners to delegate in the same manner as trustees, but the requirements as to notice are different. They are as follows:

- *Personal representatives*: notice must be given to each of the other personal representatives, if any, except any executor who has renounced probate.

- *Tenants for life*: notice must be given to the trustees of the settlement and to each person, if any, who – together with the person giving the notice – constitutes the tenant for life.

- *Statutory owners*: notice must be given to each person, if any, who – together with the person giving the notice – constitutes the statutory owner. If there is no tenant for life, any person of full age on whom such powers are by the settlement expressed to be conferred has the powers of the tenant for life (s 23(1)(a) Settled Land Act 1925). In this situation, notice must also be given to the trustees of the settlement.

6. Companies

Companies can grant powers of attorney. Section 38(1) Companies Act 1985 provides that a company may, by writing under its common seal, empower any person, either generally or in respect of any specified matters, as its attorney, to execute deeds on its behalf in any place elsewhere than in the United Kingdom. Subsection (2) provides that a deed signed by such an attorney on behalf of the company and under his seal binds the company and has the same effect as if it were under the company's common seal.

Section 35 Companies Act 1985, as amended by the Companies Act 1989 which came into force on 1 July 1990, provides that the validity of an act done by a company will not be called into question on the ground of lack of capacity by reason of anything in the company's memorandum. Section 35A(1) provides that in favour of a person dealing with a company in good faith, the power of the board of directors to bind the company, or authorise others to do so, will be deemed to be free of any limitation under the company's constitution. Under s 35A(2)(b) a person will not be regarded as acting in bad faith by reason only of his knowing that an act is beyond the powers of the directors under the company's constitution. Section 35A(2)(c) provides that a person will be presumed to have acted in good faith unless the contrary is proved. Section 35B provides that a party to a transaction with a company is not bound to enquire (i) as to whether the transaction is permitted by the company's memorandum or (ii) as to any limitation on the powers of the board of directors to bind the company or authorise others to do so. Article 71 of Table A provides:

'The directors may, by power of attorney or otherwise, appoint any person to be the agent of the company for such purposes and on such conditions as they determine, including authority for the agent to delegate all or any of his powers.'

The effect of these provisions is that a third party can deal safely with an attorney appointed by a company, unless the third party is acting in bad faith; the mere knowledge that an act is beyond the powers of the directors does not mean that the third party is acting in bad faith.

(For a more detailed discussion of this section, readers are referred to more specialist works on the subject, such as *Tolley's Company Law*.)

7. Administrators, administrative receivers and liquidators

Schedule 1 para 11 Insolvency Act 1986 authorises an administrator or administrative receiver to appoint an agent to do any business which he is unable to do himself or which can more conveniently be done by an agent.

Schedule 4 Pt III para 12 authorises a liquidator to appoint an agent to do any business which the liquidator is unable to do himself.

Within the limits of these powers, administrators, administrative receivers, and liquidators can appoint attorneys.

8. Trustees in bankruptcy

A trustee in bankruptcy can execute a power of attorney (s 314(5) and Sch 5 para 14 Insolvency Act 1986).

9. Public authorities

These are statutory creations, and have only the powers conferred by the statute creating them. Section 101(1) Local Government Act 1972 provides:

'Subject to any express provision contained in this Act or any Act passed after this Act, a local authority may arrange for the discharge of any of their functions –

(a) by a committee, a sub-committee or an officer of the authority.'

Section 111(1) provides:

'... a local authority shall have power to do anything (whether or not involving the expenditure, borrowing or lending of money or the acquisition of or disposal of any property or rights which is calculated to facilitate, or is conducive or incidental to, the discharge of any of their functions'.

A local authority can thus grant a power of attorney to an officer of the authority; possibly s 111(1) permits the grant of a power of attorney to an independent third party, provided the grant was calculated to facilitate, or was conducive or incidental to, the discharge of the functions of the local authority, although there may be limits on the powers which can be delegated. Readers are referred to more specialised works for a discussion on this topic.

10. Drunkards

If a donor, when granting a power of attorney, is so drunk as not to know what he is doing, the grant is at least voidable, and may be void. In *Gore v Gibson* (1845) 13 M & W 623, 153 ER 260 at page 626, 262 Parke B said:

'But where the party, when he enters into the contract, is in such a state of drunkenness as not to know what he is doing, and particularly when it appears that this was known to the other party, the contract is void altogether, and he cannot be compelled to perform it.'

On sobering up, however, the donor can ratify the power. Ratification is discussed in Chapter 8.

11. Enemy aliens

A person who lives or carries on business in an enemy state cannot appoint an attorney to act for him in the United Kingdom (*O'Mealey v Wilson and Another* (1808) 1 Camp 482, 170 ER 1029 and *M'Connell v Hector* (1802) 3 Bos & P 113, 127 ER 61). However, a citizen of an enemy country, who neither lives nor carries on business there, can appoint an attorney to act for him in the United Kingdom.

In *Hangkam Kwintong Woo v Lin Lan Fong* [1951] 2 All ER 567 the donor of a power of attorney lived in Hong Kong, which at the time was in the occupation of the Japanese. After the donor of the power had left Hong Kong, the donee sold a house belonging to the donor. It was held that the power was still in existence at the date of the sale. In delivering the judgment of the Privy Council, Lord Simonds said at page 572:

'The result seems plainly to ensue that, whatever consequences may follow outside the occupied territory if one of its inhabitants, who has left it, seeks to maintain or to initiate relations with another who has stayed within it, yet the courts of that country cannot regard either him who has left or him who has stayed behind as enemies of the King or enemies of each other.'

12. Duress

If a person is compelled to sign a power of attorney by force or threat of force, it will be void so far as the donor and donee are concerned (*Alexander Baton v Alexander Ewan Armstrong and Others* [1976] AC 104). The positions of third parties dealing with an attorney acting under a power tainted with duress is unclear; if the third party is innocent of any wrongdoing, the transaction may bind the donor, although the attorney will be liable in damages to the donor (see Chapter 11).

Force or threat of force to a near relative may also be sufficient to invalidate a power, but duress to goods is probably not sufficient. In *Pao On v Lau Yiu Long* [1979] 3 All ER 65 at page 79 Lord Scarman said:

'It is doubtful, however, whether at common law any duress other than duress to the person sufficed to render a contract voidable ...'

Economic duress may also invalidate a power. In *Pao On v Lau Yiu Long* Lord Scarman stated at page 79:

'In their Lordship's view, there is nothing contrary to principle in recognising economic duress as a factor which may render a contract voidable, provided always that the basis of such recognition is that it must amount to a coercion of will, which vitiates consent. It must be shown that the payment made or the contract entered into was not a voluntary act.'

In *Atlas Express Ltd v Kafco (Importers and Distributors) Ltd* [1989] 1 All ER 641 the plaintiffs were carriers, and they agreed to carry basketware for the defendants at a price of £1.10 per carton. They then demanded a minimum of £440 per load. The defendants were unable to find an alternative carrier, and had to agree to the minimum charge in order to save a contract with a retail chain. It was held that the consent was vitiated by economic duress.

If a creditor forces a debtor to give him a power of attorney by threatening to make the debtor bankrupt, it is probable that the power will be invalid.

13. Undue influence

Powers of attorney will frequently be granted in family situations, and it may be that the 'attorney' will use undue influence to procure the execution of a power in his favour. If the power is tainted with undue influence, it can be set aside, and any transaction in favour of the attorney is also liable to be set aside.

What constitutes undue influence? In *Allcard v Skinner* (1887) 36 Ch D 145 at page 171, Cotton LJ said:

'The question is – Does the case fall within the principles laid down by the decisions of the Court of Chancery in setting aside voluntary gifts executed by the parties who at the time were under such influence as, in the opinion of the court, enabled the donor afterwards to set the gift aside? These decisions may be divided into two classes – First, where the court has been satisfied that the gift was the result of influence expressly used by the donee for the purpose; second, where the relations between the donor and donee have at or shortly before the execution of the gift been such as to raise a presumption that the donee had influence over the donor. In such a case the court sets aside the voluntary gift, unless it is proved that in fact the gift was the spontaneous act of the donor acting under circumstances which enabled him to exercise an independent will and which justifies the court in holding that the gift was the result of a free exercise of the donor's will. The first class of case may be considered as depending on the principle that no one shall be allowed to retain any benefit arising from his fraud or wrongful act. In the second class of cases the court interferes, not on the ground that any wrongful act has been committed by the donee, but on the ground of public policy, and to prevent the relations which existed between the parties and the influence arising therefrom being abused.'

In *Bank of Credit and Commerce International SA v Aboody* [1992] 4 All ER 955 at 964 the Court of Appeal adopted the following classification:

Class 1: actual undue influence.

Class 2: presumed undue influence, which can be subdivided into:

Class 2a: relationships where there is a presumption of undue influence, for example solicitor and client.

Class 2b: relationships not within class 2a, but where the complainant proves the *de facto* existence of a relationship under which the complainant generally reposed trust and confidence in the wrongdoer, the existence of such a relationship raises the presumption of undue influence.

In the House of Lords case, *Barclays Bank plc v O'Brien* [1993] 4 All ER 417, Lord Browne-Wilkinson referred to the classification described above, and went on to discuss the effect of undue influence on third parties. If the third party had actual or constructive notice of the undue influence, then any transaction affecting the third party could be set aside. Presumably if undue influence is used to persuade a donor to grant a power, any transaction with a third party will be voidable if the third party is aware or should have been aware of the undue influence.

14. Fraud

If a donor is fraudulently induced to execute a power of attorney, for example, by a misrepresentation that the power is another document, or by a misrepresentation as to its effect, any transactions benefiting the donee can be set aside. Transactions between innocent third parties and a donee acting under a power tainted with fraud may not be set aside, although the attorney will be liable in damages to the donor.

II. Capacity of donor to grant an enduring power

1. Minors

The rules appear to be the same as for ordinary powers. The Law Commission, in its report on *The Incapacitated Principal* (Law Com No 122 Cmnd 8977) stated at page 22 that infants could grant enduring powers.

2. Mentally disordered persons

It may be that different tests apply to ordinary powers and enduring powers of attorney. In *Re K*; *Re F* [1988] 1 All ER 358 donors executed enduring powers. At the time when they executed the powers, both donors were verging on mental incapacity to manage their own affairs, but they understood the nature and effect of the enduring power. Hoffmann J held that both powers were valid. He pointed out that the EPAA 1985 did not specify the mental capacity needed to execute a power of attorney. A power of attorney is normally revoked by the subsequent mental incapacity of the donor (see Chapters 6 and 7), but Hoffmann J rejected the view that a person suffering from mental incapacity which would have revoked a power could not validly create one. He said at pages 362, 363:

'In practice it is likely that many enduring powers will be executed when symptoms of mental incapacity have begun to manifest themselves. These symptoms may result in the donor being mentally incapable in the statutory sense that she is unable on a regular basis to manage her property and affairs. But, as in the case of Mrs. F, she may execute the power with full understanding and with the intention of taking advantage of the Act to have her affairs managed by an attorney of her choice rather than having them put in the hands of the Court of Protection. I can think of no reason of policy why this intention should be frustrated.'

He then went on to define what degree of understanding is involved. He said:

'Plainly one cannot expect that the donor should have been able to pass an examination on the provisions of the 1985 Act. At the other extreme, I do not think that it would be sufficient if he realised only that it gave [the donee of the power] power to look after his property. Counsel as *amicus curiae* helpfully summarised the matters which the donor should have understood in order that he can be said to have understood the nature and effect of the power: first, if such be the terms of the power, that the attorney will be able to assume complete authority over the donor's affairs; second, if such be the terms of the power, that the attorney will in general be able to do anything with the donor's property which the donor could have done; third, that the authority will continue if the donor should be or become mentally incapable; fourth, that if he should be or become mentally incapable, the power will be irrevocable without confirmation by the court.'

It is uncertain whether a similar test is applicable to ordinary powers; they are of course different in that there are considerable safeguards in the EPAA 1985 which do not apply to ordinary powers.

3. Trustees

Section 2(8) EPAA 1985 provides that a power of attorney under s 25 Trustee Act 1925 cannot be an enduring power. However, s 3(3) EPAA 1985 authorises an attorney under a general or limited enduring power to execute or exercise, without obtaining any consent, all or any of the trusts, powers or discretions vested in the donor as trustee. The attorney may also give a valid receipt for capital or other money paid without the concurrence of any other person. These powers are subject to any conditions and restrictions contained in the instrument creating the power of attorney. RT Oerton in an article in the *Solicitors' Journal* (10 January 1986) points out at page 23 that this provision did not form part of the original proposals of the Law Commission, and that its effect is very wide. The author highlights the following features:

'Firstly, it delegates the donor's trustee functions whether he intends it or not ...

Secondly, this result ensues whether the EPA is "general or limited" ...

Thirdly, it enables the attorney to exercise the trustee functions "without obtaining any consent" ...

Fourthly, unlike s 25, it contains no prohibition on the appointment as attorney of an individual who is the donor's only co-trustee ...

Fifthly, it enables a trustee "without the concurrence of any other person" to "give a valid receipt for capital or other money paid" ...

Sixthly, there is no limit to the duration of the power ...

Seventhly, there is no requirement, as there is in s 25, for notice to be given to the other trustees, who may remain in complete ignorance of the power ...'

In *Powers of Attorney* (Longman, 8th edition, 1991) by Aldridge, with reference to s 22 Law of Property Act 1925 the author argues that a trustee for sale may cease to hold office if he becomes mentally incapable, and therefore in that situation any attorney cannot exercise the trustee powers vested in the donor. This view has been challenged on the ground that the EPAA 1985 has impliedly repealed the earlier provision ((1987) 131 SJ 1509 and (1995) 92/12 *Law Society's Gazette* 22 March).

4. Joint tenants or tenants in common

If an enduring power has been granted, s 3(3) EPAA 1985 authorises the donee *inter alia* to execute any of the trusts vested in the donor. A trustee who holds land on trust for joint tenants or tenants in common, and who grants an enduring power, will confer authority on the attorney to exercise his powers as trustee. A co-trustee can be appointed, and that co-trustee can give a valid receipt for capital money. It is believed that enduring powers are frequently granted in this situation, but RT Oerton has argued that an enduring power of attorney granted solely for the purpose of exercising trustee powers vested in the donor may be invalid (see *Butterworth's Wills, Probate and Administration Service* volume 1 Introduction paragraphs 364–366). However, it seems safe to continue the practice of trustees delegating their powers by granting enduring powers, although practitioners should be aware that there could be problems.

5. Personal representatives, tenants for life and statutory owners

There is nothing in the EPAA 1985 dealing specifically with the question of whether the donee of an enduring power can exercise the powers of a donor in his capacity as a personal representative. This topic is discussed in Chapter 13.

If a donor is a tenant for life or statutory owner, he or she is a trustee (ss 107(1) and 16(1) Settled Land Act 1925). Section 3(3) EPAA 1985 is probably wide enough to permit the donee to exercise the powers enjoyed by the donor as tenant for life or statutory owner.

6. Companies

A company cannot create an enduring power of attorney – it is only individuals who can do so (s 1(1) EPAA 1985).

7. Administrators, administrative receivers, liquidators and trustees in bankruptcy

It is arguable that s 3(3) EPAA 1985 permits the donee to exercise any powers vested in the donor as an administrator, administrative receiver, liquidator or trustee in bankruptcy.

8. Public authorities

A public authority cannot grant an enduring power.

9. Drunkards, enemy aliens, duress, undue influence and fraud

The rules are the same as for ordinary powers. Under s 8(4)(e) and (f) EPAA 1985 the court must cancel a registration on being satisfied that the power was not a valid and subsisting power when registration was effected, or on being satisfied that fraud or undue pressure was used to induce the donor to create the power.

III. Void powers of attorney – third party rights

1. Ordinary powers

If the power of attorney is void, for example because of mental incapacity, or because the donor is an enemy alien, any transaction entered into by the attorney will also be void. In *Daily Telegraph Newspaper Company Ltd v McLaughlin* [1904] AC 777, P executed a power of attorney whilst of unsound mind. Acting under the authority, the donee executed a transfer of shares. The High Court of Australia held that the power was void, and the transfer a nullity. The Privy Council declined to grant leave to appeal. Lord Macnaghten said at page 779:

'After careful review of the facts the High Court, differing from the judge of first instance, came to the conclusion that when the plaintiff executed the power of attorney in question he had no knowledge of what he was doing, except that he knew that he was signing his name, which under the circumstances was as described by Dr. Lamrock, who was his medical attendant, 'a mere mechanical act'. Having come to this conclusion on the facts of the case, the High Court held that the power of attorney was void, and the deed of transfer a nullity. Now the petitioners, as their Lordships understand, do not propose to contest the finding of the High Court on the question of fact, nor indeed would their Lordships be disposed to advise His Majesty to admit an appeal on such a question.'

At page 780 it was stated:

'Now, if the power of attorney is mere waste paper, it is difficult to see how anything which rests on it as the foundation and groundwork of the whole superstructure can be of any validity, whether the transaction is beneficial to the lunatic or not. The risk to a company acting on a power of attorney is, no doubt, considerable, but the directors can protect themselves to some extent by making inquiries – a precaution not apparently taken in this case.'

This quotation highlights the point that there is very little protection for a person dealing with an attorney under a void power. This topic is discussed in more detail in Chapter 12.

2. Enduring powers

The basic rule is the same as for ordinary powers, but if the power is registered, s 9 EPAA 1985 may protect a third party. Section 9 is discussed in detail in Chapter 12.

IV. Capacity of donee

Donees of ordinary powers of attorney do not need to have capacity themselves (see *Re D'Angibou; Andrews v Andrews* (1880) 15 Ch D 228 CA), but clearly it is very unwise to appoint an infant or mentally disordered person or drunkard or bankrupt as an attorney.

However, an agent lacking capacity will be liable to the principal or the third party only in so far as the agent would have been liable if the contract had been made in his personal capacity (*Smally v Smally* (1700) 1 Eq Ca Abr 6, 21 ER 831, and see *Law of Agency* (Sweet & Maxwell, 16th edition, 1996) by Bowstead and Reynolds at page 41). For example, a person suffering from mental disorder cannot enter into a valid contract, and will not therefore be liable either to the third party or to his principal. At common law, contracts entered into by infants are voidable at the option of the infant, although they bind the other party. A similar rule applies to contracts entered into by agents who are infants.

If it is intended to grant an enduring power of attorney, s 2(7) EPAA 1985 provides that a power of attorney cannot be an enduring power unless, when he executes the instrument creating it, the attorney is:

(a)   an individual who has attained eighteen years and is not bankrupt; or

(b)   a trust corporation.

Section 13(1) EPAA 1985 defines 'trust corporation' as meaning the Public Trustee or a corporation either appointed by the High Court or the county court (according to their respective jurisdictions) in any particular case to be a trustee or entitled by rules under s 4(3) Public Trustee Act 1906 to act as custodian trustee.

If joint attorneys are appointed, the reference to the time when the attorney executes the instrument is to be read as a reference to the time when the second or last attorney executes the instrument (Sch 3 Pt I para 1).

Summary

- Infants can grant powers of attorney, but will be bound by contracts entered into by the donee only if the infant would have been liable if he or she had entered into them personally.

- Mentally disordered persons, drunkards, and enemy aliens cannot grant powers of attorney.

- Trustees, personal representatives, companies, administrators, administrative receivers, liquidators, trustees in bankruptcy, and public authorities can all grant powers of attorney, although there may be limitations on their power to do so. Only individuals can grant enduring powers of attorney.

- Duress, undue influence, and fraud may invalidate a power.

- Donees of a power need not have capacity themselves, but an infant and a bankrupt cannot be an attorney under an enduring power.

Chapter 10

Duties and rights of donees

Frequently, the grant of a power of attorney is a family affair where the donor does not expect to remunerate the donee, the donee does not expect to be remunerated by the donor, and neither party intends to enter into a contractual arrangement. This will usually be the case when a parent grants a power of attorney to his or her child, or a spouse grants a power to the other spouse. However, if a client asks a professional person like a solicitor or accountant to act as attorney, there will almost invariably be a contract between the donor and the donee of the power.

Both paid and unpaid attorneys owe similar duties to the donor of the power, although the duties do differ in certain minor respects, and in one major respect.

It should be stressed that if there is a contract between parties, the duties of the parties will depend on the express or implied terms of that contract. The courts are reluctant to imply terms into a contract; in *Lazarus v Cairn Line of Steamships Ltd* (1912) 106 LT 378 Scrutton J at page 380 stated:

> 'I read them (the earlier authorities) as deciding (1) that the first thing to consider is the express words the parties have used; (2) that a term they have not expressed is not to be implied because the court thinks it is a reasonable term, but only if the court thinks it is necessarily implied in the nature of the contract the parties have made.'

Despite this reluctance to imply terms into a contract, it is more than likely that terms will have to be implied. If a solicitor or accountant is appointed to act as attorney by a client, it is possible that the parties will not agree any express terms.

I. Duties of donees of ordinary powers

1. To act

It is this aspect where there is a major difference between a donee under a contract, and a donee who is not acting pursuant to any contract.

A donee who is not acting under any contract does not have to act under the power of attorney. Of course, the donor and donee will often be related in this situation, and the donee will usually want to exercise the power.

However, a donee who is acting under a contract may be under a contractual duty to act. Whether the donee is or is not under such a duty depends on the express or implied terms of the contract between the donor and donee. If a client gives a solicitor or an accountant a power of attorney, there will usually be a duty on the solicitor or accountant to act.

The question of termination of powers of attorney is discussed in Chapter 6, but if the donee is under a contractual obligation to act, the donee may have to continue acting until the contractual obligation has been discharged.

2. Utmost good faith to the donor

In *Rothschild v Brookman* (1831) 2 Dow & Cl 188, 6 ER 699, at page 198, 703, Lord Wynford said:

> '... and I think it fit that your Lordships should say, in language which cannot be misunderstood, that in these transactions of trust and confidence there must be, on the part of the person trusted, that most marked integrity, that *uberrimae fides*, which cannot leave a doubt as to the fairness of the transaction'.

Many of the duties discussed in this chapter are illustrations of this rule, but for convenience they are dealt with separately.

3. To keep accounts

It is essential that the attorney keeps accurate accounts and records. In *Gray v Haig* (1855) 20 Beav 219, 52 ER 587, Sir John Romilly MR said at pages 238 and 239, 594 and 595:

> 'It cannot, however, be too generally known or understood, amongst all persons dealing with each other, in the character

of principal and agent, how severely the court deals with any irregularities on the part of the agent, how strictly it requires that he who is the person trusted shall act, in all matters relating to such agency, for the benefit of his principal, and how imperative it is upon him to preserve correct accounts of all his dealings and transactions in that respect, and that the loss and still more destruction of such evidence, by the agent, falls most heavily upon himself.'

An attorney who is a solicitor will of course be bound by the Solicitors' Accounts Rules, and will in any event have to keep accurate records. However, a lay attorney should also keep accurate records. Relatives who are appointed attorneys are under a similar duty (*Dadswell v Jacobs* (1887) 34 Ch D 278).

If the attorney combines the property of the donor with his own so that it is not possible to determine what belongs to the donor, the whole will be taken to belong to the donor (*Lupton v White* (1808) 15 Ves 432, 33 ER 817). Thus it is undesirable for an attorney to combine his own money with the donor's in one bank or building society account; ideally, there should be a separate account for the money belonging to the donor.

4. To disclose all relevant facts in certain transactions

The donee of a power of attorney is not prohibited from purchasing the property of the donor of the power, or selling his own property to the donor, provided that he makes full disclosure of all material facts (*Dunne v English* (1874) LR 18 Eq 524 and *Armstrong v Jackson* [1917] 2 KB 822). In *Dunne v English*, Sir George Jessel MR said at page 533:

'It is not enough for an agent to tell the principal that he is going to have an interest in the purchase, or to have a part in the purchase. He must tell him all the material facts. He must make full disclosure.'

In *McPherson v Watt* (1877) 3 App Cas 254 HL, a Scottish advocate purchased property belonging to two ladies for whom he was agent in the name of his brother. Lord O'Hagan listed at page 266 the requirements for such a transaction to be upheld; the agent must be able to show that:

(a) he has acted with the most complete faithfulness and fairness;

(b) his advice has been free from all taint of self-interest;

(c) he has not misrepresented or concealed anything;

(d) he has given an adequate price;

(e) his client has had the advantage of the best professional assistance which, if he had been engaged in a transaction with a third party, he could possibly have afforded;

(f) if the purchase is to be made in the name of another, this fact has been disclosed.

Similar principles govern the following transactions between the donor and donee of a power of attorney:

- loan of money by donor to donee;
- loan of money by donee to donor;
- the grant of a mortgage by the donor to the donee;
- the grant of a mortgage by the donee to the donor;
- the grant of a lease by the donor to the donee;
- the grant of a lease by the donee to the donor.

This is not an exclusive list, and there may be other transactions which are governed by the same principles.

Even after the power of attorney has terminated, the donee may still be under a duty to disclose all relevant facts. In *Alison v Clayhills* (1907) 97 LT 709 Parker J at page 711 said:

'It appears to me to be quite clear that a solicitor is not wholly incapacitated from purchasing or taking a lease from his client, but, where the relationship of solicitor and client exists, the onus of upholding the vitality of such a transaction will rest upon the solicitor. It is, I think, equally clear that although the relationship of solicitor and client in its strict sense has been discontinued, the same principle applies as long as the confidence naturally arising from such a relationship is proved or may be presumed to continue.'

5. Not to make secret profits

In *Turnbull v Garden* (1869) 38 LJ Ch 331 at page 334 James V-C said:

'What appears in this case shows the danger of allowing even the smallest departure from the rule that a person who is dealing with another man's money ought to give the truest account of what he has done, and ought not to receive anything in the nature of a present or allowance without the full knowledge of the principal that he is so acting.'

An attorney must therefore disclose to the donee of the power any profits or commissions which he receives as a consequence of the agency, or as a consequence of the use of trust property, or as a consequence of the use of confidential information acquired as agent. For example, if the attorney insures the property of the donor, and receives commission from the insurance company, he would have to disclose this commission to the donor of the power. Even if full disclosure is made, the attorney may still have to account for the commission unless the donor agrees that the attorney can retain it. However, if the donor delays taking action to recover secret profits, the agent will be allowed to keep them. In *Great Western Insurance Co v Cunliffe* (1874) LR 9 Ch App 525 an insurance company in New York appointed a firm of merchants in London as its agents. The agents arranged reinsurance, and were paid a commission of 5 per cent, and in addition 12 per cent of certain profits. The insurance company discovered what was happening in 1866, but did not object until 1868. It was held that it could not recover the commissions.

6. Not to exceed the authority conferred by the power

If the donor has conferred a general power on the attorney, the donee can do anything which the donor could have lawfully done (see s 10(1) Powers of Attorney Act 1971). If the donor has conferred only a limited power on the donee, for example to sell a particular property for not less than a fixed price, the donee must ensure that he acts within the limitations of the power, and sells the property for not less than the fixed price. The donee must not rely on the courts giving a liberal interpretation as limited powers of attorney are construed strictly (see Chapter 8).

7. To take care and be skilful

Whether or not the grant of a power of attorney has created a contractual relationship, the donee of the power is under a duty to discharge his duties with reasonable care. The standard of care required depends on the qualifications of the donee. In *Harmer v Cornelius* (1858) 5 CBNS 236, 141 ER 94, Willes J at pages 246, 98 said:

'When a skilled labourer, artisan, or artist is employed, there is on his own part an implied warranty that he is of skill reasonably competent to the task he undertakes ... Thus, if an apothecary, a watchmaker, or an attorney be employed for reward, they each impliedly undertake to possess and exercise reasonable skill in their several arts. The public profession of an art is a representation and undertaking to all the world that the professor possesses the requisite ability and skill.'

In *Hart & Hodge v John Frame, Son, & Co* (1839) 6 C & F 193, 7 ER 670 at pages 209, 676, the Lord Chancellor stated:

'Professional men, possessed of a reasonable portion of information and skill, according to the duties they undertake to perform and exercising what they so possess with reasonable care and diligence in the affairs of their employers, certainly ought not to be held liable for errors in judgement, whether in matters of law or discretion. Every case, therefore, ought to depend on its own peculiar circumstances; and when an injury has been sustained which could not have arisen except from the want of such reasonable skill and diligence, or the absence of the employment of either on the part of the attorney, the law holds him liable.'

Thus a far higher standard of care will be expected from a solicitor or accountant than an unqualified person.

It may be that there is a different test for gratuitous donees. In *Beal v South Devon Railway Company* (1864) 3 H & C 337, 159 ER 560 Crompton J said at pages 341, 562:

'What is reasonable varies in the case of a gratuitous bailee and that of a bailee for hire. From the former is reasonably expected such care and diligence as persons ordinarily use in their own affairs, and such skill as he has. From the latter is reasonably expected care and diligence, such as are exercised in the ordinary and proper course of similar business and such skill as he ought to have, namely the skill usual and requisite in the business for which he receives payment.'

A solicitor who is the donee of a power of attorney, and who is paid, must exercise the skill of a reasonably competent solicitor, but if he is unpaid and is usually incompetent as a solicitor, he need exercise only the skill he applies to his own affairs and the skill he exercises as an incompetent solicitor.

If the donee has a discretion, for example to choose an insurance company with which to insure the donor's property, or an auctioneer to sell it, he will not be liable provided he acts in a *bona fide* manner (*Moore v Mourge* (1776) 2 Cowp 479, 98 ER 1197).

II. Duties of donees of enduring powers

The duties of donees of enduring powers of attorney are by and large the same as the duties imposed on donees of ordinary powers. However, there is one additional duty imposed on the donees of enduring powers, which is to register the power. If an attorney under an enduring power of attorney has reason to believe that the donor is or is becoming mentally incapable, the attorney must, as soon as practicable, make an application to the court for the registration of the instrument creating the power (s 4(1) and (2) EPAA 1985). This requirement of registration is discussed in Chapter 7.

The EPAA 1985 sometimes imposes extra requirements, and these will now be considered.

1. To act

Unless there is a contractual obligation to do so, there is no obligation on the donee of an enduring power to act. However, if the donee is under a duty to apply for registration of the power, no disclaimer of the power is valid unless and until the attorney gives notice of it to the court (s 4(6)); similarly, once the power is registered, no disclaimer of the power is valid unless and until the attorney gives notice of it to the court.

The procedural requirements are discussed in Chapter 7.

2. Utmost good faith to the donor

The same duty applies to the donee of an enduring power and the donee of an ordinary power.

3. To keep accounts

The same duty applies to the donee of an enduring power and the donee of an ordinary power.

Once a power is registered, under s 8(2)(b)(ii) EPAA 1985 the court may give directions with respect to the rendering of accounts by the attorney and the production of records kept by him for the purpose, and under s 8(2)(c) the court may require the attorney to furnish information or produce documents or things in his possession as attorney.

4. To disclose all relevant facts in certain transactions

The donee of an enduring power is under the same duty as the donee of an ordinary power.

Once an enduring power has been registered, the court in effect stands in the shoes of the donor, and under s 8(2)(b)(i) EPAA 1985 the court may give directions with respect to the management or disposal by the attorney of the property and affairs of the donor. Under s 8(2)(d) the court may give any consent or authorisation to act which the attorney would have to obtain from a mentally capable donor, and under s 8(2)(e) the court may authorise the attorney to act so as to benefit himself or other persons than the donor (but subject to any conditions and restrictions contained in the instrument).

Thus if the donee of an enduring power, which has been registered, wants to enter into some transaction concerning the property of the donor, for example, purchasing or leasing property belonging to the donor, he must obtain the consent of the court.

It should be noted that if the power is not registered, the donee need not obtain the consent of the court.

5. Not to make secret profits

The same duty applies to the donee of an enduring power as to the donee of an ordinary power. Once the power is registered, s 8 EPAA 1985 applies. Section 8(2)(d) provides that the court may give any consent or authorisation to act which the attorney would have to obtain from a mentally capable donor, and s 8(2)(e) permits the court to authorise the attorney to act so as to benefit himself or persons other than the donor.

Thus if the donee of a registered enduring power wants to receive any profit or commission as a consequence of the agency, he must obtain the consent of the court. There is no such need, however, if the power is not registered.

6. Not to exceed the authority conferred by the power

If an enduring power confers a general authority on the attorney, under s 3(2) EPAA 1985 it confers on the attorney authority to do on behalf of the donor anything which the donor can lawfully do by attorney. This is subject to the restriction imposed in subs (5) with regard to gifts.

If a limited power is conferred, the donee must not exceed the authority conferred, and it is unwise to rely upon the courts giving the power a liberal interpretation.

Once the power is registered, s 7(1)(c) EPAA 1985 provides that the donor may not extend or restrict the scope of the authority, and any instruction or consent given by the donor is ineffective. However, under s 8(2)(d) the court can given any consent or authorisation to act which the attorney would have to obtain from a mentally capable donor, and under s 8(2)(f) the court can relieve the attorney wholly or partly from any liability which he has or may have on account of a breach of his duties as attorney. In the light of the restricted interpretation placed upon s 8 in *Re R* [1990] 2 WLR 1219, it may be that the court will give these subsections a limited interpretation. It seems unlikely that a court will be prepared to authorise an act completely outside the power originally conferred on the donee.

7. To take care and be skilful

The same duty applies to donees under both ordinary and enduring powers.

Section 8(1)(f) enables the court to relieve the attorney wholly or partly from any liability which he has or may have incurred on account of a breach of his duties as attorney.

III. Rights of donees of ordinary powers

1. Indemnity

The donee may incur expenses in exercising the powers conferred by a power of attorney. If the donor and donee of the power are related, the donee may be prepared to meet these expenses himself. If he is not prepared to do so, there will usually be an implied right to an indemnity if one is not expressly given by the power. In *Adamson v Jarvis* (1827) 4 Bing 66, 130 ER 693, Best CJ at pages 72, 695 said:

> '... every man who employs another to do an act which the employer appears to have a right to authorise to do undertakes to indemnify him for all such acts as would be lawful if the employer had the authority he pretends to have'.

If there is an express right of indemnity, it may extend to payments which the agent is liable to make, but for which the principal is not liable. In *Adams v Morgan and Company Ltd* [1924] 1 KB 751, P sold a business to D, a company. It was agreed that P would carry on the business as D's agent, but that he would be entitled to an indemnity. P incurred a liability for supertax in respect of the period during which he carried on the business as D's agent. It was held that P was entitled to be indemnified against this supertax even though companies were not liable for supertax.

There is no right to an indemnity, however, if the agent exceeds his authority (*Barron v Fitzgerald* (1840) 6 Bing NS 201, 133 ER 79). Similarly, there will be no right to an indemnity if neither the agent nor the principal is under any legal liability (*Owen v Tate* [1976] 1 QB 402). In addition, the expense must be reasonable.

2. Remuneration

Whether an agent is entitled to remuneration depends on whether there is any express or implied term in a contract to the effect that the attorney should be paid. Most powers of attorney do not contain any express term about payment; therefore most donees will have to rely upon an implied term if they want payment. In what circumstances will the courts imply a term so as to give an attorney a right to remuneration? In *Way v Latilla* [1937] 3 All ER 759 Lord Atkin said at page 763:

'But, while there is, therefore, no concluded contract as to the remuneration, it is plain that there existed between the parties a contract of employment under which Mr. Way was engaged to do work for Mr. Latilla in circumstances which clearly indicated the work was not to be gratuitous.'

If a donor appoints a solicitor or accountant as his attorney, there will usually be an implied agreement that the donee should be remunerated. On the other hand, if a relative of the donor is appointed as attorney, the courts will probably say that the circumstances are not such as would entitle the attorney to be paid, unless of course the relative was in practice as a solicitor or accountant.

Even if there is no contract, the court may be prepared to order remuneration on a *quantum meruit* basis. In *Craven-Ellis v Canons Ltd* [1936] 2 KB 403 the contract between P and a company was void. It was held that P was entitled to recover on a *quantum meruit* basis. Greer LJ said at page 409:

'The contract, having been made by directors who had no authority to make it with one of themselves who had notice of their want of authority, was not binding on either party. It was, in fact, a nullity, and presents no obstacle to the implied promise to pay on a quantum meruit basis which arises from the performance of the services and the implied acceptance of the same by the company.'

Before the court will order payment on a *quantum meruit* basis, there must thus be a performance of services and an acceptance of those services.

What guidelines will the court use in fixing the amount of remuneration? The court will award a reasonable amount as remuneration, and will have regard to any trade usage (*Way v Latilla*). Solicitors will therefore be entitled to charge on their usual basis, provided of course that that is reasonable.

If the donee exceeds his authority, or is guilty of a breach of duty, he will not be entitled to any remuneration (*Marsh v Jelf* (1862) 3 F 6 F 234, 176 ER 105).

IV. Rights of donees of enduring powers

1. Indemnity and remuneration

In an article in the *Solicitors' Journal* (20 June 1986) RT Oerton argues at page 458 that s 3 EPAA 1985, which deals with the scope of the authority of an attorney under an enduring power, does not specifically authorise an attorney to charge. However, the author considers that s 8(2)(b)(iii) of the Act may resolve the problem.

Section 8(2)(b)(iii) EPAA 1985 empowers the court to give directions with respect to the remuneration or expenses of the attorney, whether or not in default of or in accordance with any provision made by the instrument, including directions for the repayment of excessive remuneration, or the payment of additional remuneration. This clearly contemplates that an attorney under an enduring power can be paid,

On the assumption that an attorney under an enduring power is entitled to be paid, it seems that the law which is applicable to ordinary powers as regards indemnity and remuneration applies also to enduring powers.

V. Liens

A lien is the right to retain property belonging to another person who owes money to the person in possession of the property. It may be that the donee of both an ordinary power of attorney and an enduring power will have a lien on property which belongs to the donor and which is in the possession of the donee. This lien must either be given by the general law or by contract (*Gladstone v Birley* (1817) 2 Mer 401, 35 ER 993).

At common law solicitors have a lien on property, funds, documents and papers belonging to a client which are in their possession for moneys due to the solicitor. See Halsbury's *Laws of England* (4th edition) volume 44 paragraph 226 onwards.

Other donees are entitled to particular but not general liens. This means that if the donee spends money maintaining a car on behalf of the donor, the donee would be entitled to a lien on the car. However, if the donee spends money maintaining a house on behalf of the same donor, he cannot claim a lien on the car for that expenditure (*Bock v Gorrissen* (1860) 2 De GF & J 434, 45 ER 689).

VI. Solicitors and powers of attorney

1. Conflict of interests

Solicitors are frequently appointed attorneys by clients. Their relationship is governed by the general law, and in addition by the rules and principles governing the professional conduct of solicitors. The donee under a general power of attorney is in a very powerful position as regards the assets of the donor; all the assets of the donor can be sold, and different assets bought with the proceeds. Can a solicitor acting under a general power sell property to the donor, or buy property from the donor? Can such a solicitor lend money to the donor, or borrow money from the donor? Can the solicitor acting under the power of attorney invest the money of the donor in a company in which he is a majority shareholder? There is clearly a conflict of interest between the donor and the donee in these situations. In all these cases, the donor must have independent legal advice; if the donor does not obtain independent advice, the solicitor must not go on with the sale, purchase, loan or investment. Advice is not limited to legal advice; it may include the advice of a valuer as to the value of property.

A solicitor can charge the donor for the work done on behalf of the donor, provided that the solicitor would have advised the client to pay if another solicitor had rendered the bill; in other words the charges must be reasonable (see The Law Society's *Guide to the Professional Conduct of Solicitors 1996* at page 278).

2. Financial services

A solicitor who is the donee of a power of attorney may have to invest money on behalf of the donee. Such a solicitor is of course subject to the Financial Services Act 1986 and the Solicitors' Investment Business Rules 1995.

Solicitors must comply with the Solicitors' Investment Business Rules 1995. Chapter 5 contains rules which apply to all firms, and deal *inter alia* with advertisements and records. Chapter 6 contains the rules which apply to firms undertaking discrete investment business. Chapter 4 defines discrete investment business; it excludes from the definition of discretionary management the situation where no remuneration is received for the discretionary management of investments in addition to any remuneration which may be received for acting as donee of a power of attorney or receiver. The situation where the donee acts under the advice of a permitted third party is also excluded. The definition of advising excludes the situation where the recommendation is made by a trustee to a co-trustee or attorney to a co-attorney, and no remuneration is received for this in addition to any remuneration which may be received for acting as trustee or attorney. The definitions of dealing and arranging have similar exclusions.

Summary
- A gratuitous attorney is under no duty to act, but an attorney may be under a contractual obligation to do so.
- An attorney owes a duty of umost good faith to the donor.
- An attorney must keep accounts.
- An attorney may be under a duty to disclose all relevant facts.
- An attorney must not make secret profits.
- An attorney must not exceed the authority conferred by the power.

- An attorney must take care and be skilful; the degree of care and skill required depends on various factors.

- The donee under an enduring power is under similar duties, but they may be modified by the EPAA.

- The donee of an enduring power must apply for registration of the power if he has reason to believe that the donor is or is becoming mentally incapable.

- An attorney is entitled to be indemnified against all expenses properly incurred in the performance of his duties.

- An attorney may be entitled to remuneration.

- An attorney may be entitled to a lien.

- Solicitors who are attorneys can have dealings with the donee, but the donee may have to be independently advised.

- Solicitors who are attorneys must comply with the Solicitors' Investment Business Rules 1995.

Chapter 11

Rights and liabilities of donor, donee and third parties

Although many of the cases referred to relate to contracts entered into by agents not authorised under a power of attorney, the same principles usually apply to contracts entered into by the donee of a power of attorney.

I. Ordinary powers of attorney

1. Acts within the express authority of the donee

(a) Rights and liabilities of the donor

The donor of a power is bound by all acts within the express authority of the donee. The extent of the express authority conferred on the attorney must be ascertained by looking at the power, which may confer a general or limited power on the attorney.

If the act is within the express authority of the donee, the donor will be liable, even though the donee has committed some breach of duty owed to the donor. In *Hambro v Burnand* [1904] 2 KB 10, CA at page 20 Collins MR said:

> 'It would be impossible as it seems to me, for the business of a mercantile community to be carried on, if a person dealing with an agent was bound to go behind the authority of the agent in each case, and inquire whether his motive did or did not involve the application of the authority for his own private purposes.'

Although a person dealing with an attorney need not make inquiries to confirm that the attorney is acting properly, he should always check the power of attorney to make sure that it authorises the proposed transaction(s). As the courts are reluctant to imply powers, a person dealing with the attorney should ensure that there is an express power authorising the transaction.

There is some doubt as to whether a donor of a power of attorney can sue and be sued on a deed entered into by the donee. The rule at common law is that the donor can sue and be sued on the deed only if the deed states that he is a party, and the donee has executed the deed in the name of the donor (*In re International Contract Company; Pickering's claim* (1861) 6 Ch App 525 and *Berkeley v Hardy* (1826) 5 B & C 355). Equity will in appropriate circumstances hold that the donee is a trustee for the principal, and therefore the donor can enforce the trust (*Harmer v Armstrong* [1934] 1 Ch 65).

It may be that the Powers of Attorney Act 1971 has amended these rules. Section 7(1), as amended by the Law of Property (Miscellaneous Provisions) Act 1989, provides that if the donee of a power of attorney is an individual, he may, if he thinks fit:

'(a) execute any instrument with his own signature, and,

(b) do any other thing in his own name,

by the authority of the donor of the power; and any document executed or thing done in that manner shall be as effective as if executed by the donee with the signature and seal, or, as the case may be, in the name, of the donor of the power.'

In Law of Agency (16th edition) by Bowstead and Reynolds, it is stated at page 428 that there are two problems with this subsection:

(i) Should the donee have specific authority to act in his own name?

(ii) Must the principal be named in the deed?

Bowstead is of the opinion that the donee need not have specific authority to act in his name, but that the principal must be named. The authority for this second proposition is *Harmer v Armstrong*, where Lawrence LJ said at page 86:

'It is well settled and not disputed by the plaintiffs that at common law no one can sue on a contract under seal except the contracting parties.'

Bowstead concludes that:

'The effect of the section is therefore to allow execution by an attorney in his own name: but the principal should be mentioned in the body of the deed, and though it may not be strictly necessary, it is highly desirable that the attorney should express that he executes as attorney or on behalf of the principal . . .' (page 428).

Section 56(1) Law of Property Act 1925 provides that a person may take an immediate or other interest in land or other property, or the benefit of any condition, right of entry, covenant or agreement over or respecting land or other property, although he may not be named as a party to the conveyance or other instrument. The interpretation of this section is uncertain (see *Chitty on Contracts* (26th edition, Sweet & Maxwell, 1989) paragraph 1362), and it is unwise to rely on it.

(c) Rights and liabilities of the donee

If the donee discloses that he is an agent, and reveals the name of the donor, there is a contract between the donor and the third party, and the basic rule is that the donee cannot sue the third party, and cannot be sued by the third party. In *Montgomerie v UK Mutual SS Assn Ltd* [1891] 1 QB 370 at page 371 Wright J said:

'There is no doubt whatever as to the general rule as regards an agent, that where a person contracts as agent for a principal the contract is the contract of the principal, and not that of the agent; and prima facie, at common law the only person who may sue is the principal, and the only person who can be sued is the principal.'

However, the agent will not always escape liability. In *Montgomerie* Wright J said at page 371:

'To that rule there are of course many exceptions: first, the agent may be added as the party to the contract if he has so contracted, and is appointed as the party to be sued.'

At page 372 he continued:

'Also, and this is very important, in all cases the parties can by their express contract provide that the agent shall be the person liable either concurrently with or to the exclusion of the principal, or that the agent shall be the party to sue either concurrently with or to the exclusion of the principal.'

The donee of a power of attorney should therefore take care not to become a party to the contract, or to become liable jointly with the donor.

In *Bridges & Salmon v The Swan (Owner)* [1968] 1 Lloyd's Rep 5 Brandon J stated:

'Where A contracts with B on behalf of a disclosed principal C, the question whether both A and C are liable on the contract or only C depends on the intention of the parties. That intention is to be gathered from (1) the nature of the contract, (2) its terms and (3) the surrounding circumstances ... The intention for which the court looks is not the subjective intention of A or of B. Their subjective intentions may differ. The intention for which the court looks is an objective intention of both parties, based on what two reasonable businessmen making a contract of that nature, in those terms and in those surrounding circumstances, must be taken to have intended.

Where a contract is wholly in writing, the intention depends on the true construction, having regard to the nature of the contract and the surrounding circumstances, of the document or documents in which the contract is contained. Where ... the contract is partly oral and partly in writing, the intention depends on the true effect, having regard again to the nature of the contract and the surrounding circumstances, of the oral and written terms taken together.

Many of the decided cases on questions of this kind relate to contracts wholly in writing. But it seems to me that, in principle, there can be no difference in the approach to the problem whether the contract concerned is wholly in writing or partly in writing and partly oral. In either case the terms of the contract must be looked at and their true effect ascertained.'

A donee may thus become personally liable on a contract entered into on behalf of the donor if it would appear to a reasonable businessman that it was the intention of the donee to be personally liable. However, it is possible to avoid this consequence if the donee makes it '"as agent for", or "on account of", or "on behalf of", or simply "for" a principal' (Brandon J in *The Swan* at page 13). Similarly, signing as 'attorney for' will enable the donee to escape personal liability on the contract.

If the donee is personally liable, he can sue to enforce the contract (*Joseph v Knox* (1813) 3 Camp 320, 170 ER 1397).

A donee can sue on a deed if he has executed the deed using his own name, and is a party to the deed (*Appleton v Binks* (1804) 5 East 148, 102 ER 1025). It is not clear whether the donee is liable under s 7 Powers of Attorney Act 1971 (see *Law of Agency* (16th edition) by Bowstead and Reynolds at pages 428 and 587).

2. Acts within the implied or usual authority of an agent

The courts will imply into a power of attorney whatever powers are necessary to carry out the main purpose of the power; this topic was discussed in Chapter 8.

An agent may also have the authority which an agent in that position would normally have. This is known as usual authority, and in *Watteau v Fenwick* [1893] 1 QB 346 Willes J said at page 348:

'... the principal is liable for all the acts of the agent which are within the authority usually confided to an agent of that character ...'

A power of attorney may specifically authorise the donee to run a business, and a general power will include authority to do so. The donee running a business under a power of attorney will have the authority which one would expect a person running that type of business to have. Any restriction on the power in the power of attorney will not be effective unless the third party is aware of it. However, the donor will not be liable if the person dealing with the donee knew or ought to have known that the donee was exceeding his authority.

In *Reckitt v Barnett, Pembroke and Slater Ltd* [1929] AC 176 HL, a solicitor was appointed an attorney, and drew a cheque in favour of the respondents in settlement of a private debt. Viscount Dunedin said at page 184:

'... on the face of the cheque they received they saw two things (1) that it was Reckitt's account which was being drawn on, not Lord Terrington's; (2) that Lord Terrington ascribed his power to draw on that account to his position as Reckitt's attorney. The respondents made no further enquiry. They took the cheque for what it was worth ... The respondents not having made any enquiry cannot be in a better position than if they had made enquiry'.

The best procedure is for anyone who knows he is dealing with an attorney to confirm that the attorney has power to enter into the proposed transaction; if he does not, and the transaction is outside the power, the donor of the power may not be liable.

If an act is within the implied or usual authority of the donee, the rights and liabilities of the donor and donee are the same as when the act is expressly authorised.

3. Acts within the ostensible authority of an attorney

The donor of a power is liable for the acts of the attorney within the ostensible authority of the attorney (*Uxbridge Permanent Benefit Building Society v Pickard* [1939] 2 KB 248). Ostensible authority is the authority which an attorney appears to have, because the donor has held the agent out as having that authority. In *Freeman & Lockyer (A firm) v Buckhurst Park Properties (Mangal) Ltd* [1964] 2 QB 480 Diplock LJ said at page 503:

'An "apparent" or "ostensible" authority, on the other hand, is a legal relationship between the principal and the contractor created by a representation, made by the principal to the contractor, intended to be and in fact acted upon by the contractor, that the agent has authority to enter on behalf of the principal into a contract of a kind within the scope of the "apparent" authority, so as to render the principal liable to perform any obligations imposed upon him by such a contract. To the relationships so created the agent is a stranger. He need not be (although he generally is) aware of the existence of the representation, but he must not purport to make the agreement as principal for himself. The representation, when acted upon by the contractor by entering into a contract with the agent, operates as an estoppel, preventing the principal from asserting that he is not bound by the contract. It is irrelevant whether the agent had actual authority to enter into the contract.'

A person dealing with the donee of a power of attorney may not be aware that that person is acting under a power. If the donee buys goods from that person, and the donor pays for them, future purchases of those goods will be within the ostensible authority of the donee, even though they may not be expressly authorised by the power.

If an act is within the ostensible authority of the donee, the rights and liabilities of the donor and donee are identical to the rights and liabilities when the act is expressly authorised.

4. Acts outside the actual or ostensible authority of the donee

The donor of a power of attorney is not liable for acts outside the actual or ostensible authority of the donee, unless he ratifies them expressly, or accepts the benefit of the transaction (*Jacobs v Morris* [1902] 1 Ch 816). For example, if the donee buys food for the donor, which the donor eats, the donor will not be allowed to claim that the purchase is outside the authority of the donee. Ratification is discussed on page 74.

If the donee of a power of attorney borrows money without authority, and uses it to pay off debts of the donor, the lender will be able to recover the money from the donor to the extent that it was applied in paying off the debts of the donor (*Jacobs v Morris* [1902] 1 Ch 816 and *Bannatyne v D & C Maciver* [1906] 1 KB 103 CA).

If the donee has no authority, any person dealing with the donee will be able to sue the donee for breach of warranty of authority. In *Starkey v Bank of England* [1903] AC 114 HL a broker relied upon a power of attorney to arrange a transfer of stock; the broker did not know that the power of attorney was forged. It was held that the broker had impliedly warranted that he had authority, and he was liable to indemnify the Bank of England which had had to indemnify the original stockholder.

However, if the person dealing with the attorney knew that the attorney was acting without authority, the attorney will not be liable. In *Halbot v Lens* [1901] 1 Ch 344 the defendant signed a memorandum concerning an arrangement between his creditors in the following manner:

'for self and wife and Dr. Clarke'.

The plaintiff also signed the memorandum. Under it, Dr Clarke was to release all claims against the defendant. The defendant had no authority to sign for his wife or Dr Clarke, and before signing he had made it clear that he had no authority to sign for Dr Clarke. It was held that he was not liable in damages for failing to obtain the release from Dr Clarke.

5. Failure by the donee to disclose the name of the principal, or the fact of agency

If the donee of a power of attorney fails to disclose that he is acting as an attorney within his actual or implied authority, the donor can still sue and be sued on the contract. In *Teheran-Europe Co Ltd v ST Belton (Tractors) Ltd* [1968] 2 QB 545 at pages 552 and 553 Lord Denning said:

'It is a well established rule of English law that an undisclosed principal can sue and be sued upon a contract, even though his name and even his existence is undisclosed, save in those cases when the terms of the contract expressly or impliedly confine it to the parties to it. The rule is an anomaly, but is justified by business convenience. It has been held so for many years. The only question in the case is whether this rule (that an undisclosed principal can sue and be sued) extends to a case where the principal is a foreigner. In my opinion, the rule applies to a foreign principal, just as to an English principal.'

There is some doubt about the liability of an undisclosed principal if the agent is acting within the scope of his *usual* or *apparent* authority. In *Watteau v Fenwick* [1893] 1 QB 346 the defendants were brewers, and they held out their manager as being the owner of the business. The manager was forbidden to purchase certain items other than from the defendants, but in breach of this prohibition the defendant bought items from the plaintiffs. The plaintiffs discovered who was the real owner of the business, and sued for the cost of these items. It was held that the plaintiffs could sue. Willes J said at page 348:

'... once it is established that the defendant was the real principal, the ordinary doctrine of principal and agent applies – that the principal is liable for all acts of the agent which are within the authority usually confided to an agent of that character, notwithstanding limitations, as between the principal and agent put upon that authority'.

This seems to suggest that in all cases of agency, the undisclosed principal can sue and be sued, including the case where the agent is acting within the scope of his usual or apparent authority. It is uncertain whether this case is correct; for a fuller discussion, readers are referred to *Law of Agency* (7th edition, Butterworth, 1990) by Fridman at page 71 onwards and pages 265 and 266.

6. Unauthorised property transactions

The donor of a power will clearly be bound by any disposal of property within the actual, implied, usual, and ostensible authority of the donor. He will also be bound by any such disposal, even though the disposal may not have been in the manner originally contemplated, provided that the third party is not aware of this fact (*Lloyds and Scottish Finance Ltd v Williamson* [1965] 1 All ER 641).

The donor of a power will not be bound by a disposition of his property which is outside the actual, implied, usual or ostensible authority of the donee, even if the donor has been negligent (*Farquharson Brothers & Co v King & Co* [1902] AC 325 at page 336).

However, the donor may be estopped from denying that the donee had authority to sell the asset. If the donor has held the donee out as owning an asset, or as having power to sell the asset, the donor will not be allowed later on to deny that the donee could transfer a good title to the third party.

To what extent can a donee who is entrusted with property of the donor deal with it for his own benefit? For example, can a donee who is entrusted with the title deeds of a house deposit them with a bank as security for the repayment of a loan made to the donee personally? In *Brocklesby v Temperance Building Society* [1895] AC 173 the appellant was a solicitor in partnership with his son. He authorised the son to borrow money from a certain bank, and entrusted him with certain deeds relating to a mortgage and lease-hold house. The son used the deeds to borrow more money from another bank. It was held that the appellant was bound by the transaction. Lord Watson said at page 183:

'... it appears to me to be just and reasonable that, the agent having the control of the securities for the purpose of borrowing, with the consent of the principal, a lender, who has no notice to the contrary, should be entitled to deal with him on the footing that he had authority to pledge the securities to the full amount of their value'.

Thus if a donor of a power of attorney permits the donee to have possession of property or evidence of ownership, and the donee sells that property to an innocent third party, the third party may be able to defeat any claim by the donor. Similarly, if the donee uses the property to obtain a loan, the donor will have to repay the loan before the property can be recovered.

If the person dealing with the donee knows or ought to know of the lack of authority, that person may become a trustee of the property (*Reckitt v Barnett, Pembroke and Slater Ltd* [1929] AC 176 HL).

7. Effect of payment to the attorney

A third party owes money to the donor, and pays it to the donee of a power. Is the third party discharged from liability? If the donee had authority to receive the money, the third party will be discharged. Similarly, even if the donee had no authority to accept payment, if the donee pays the money received from the third party to the donor, the third party will be discharged (see *Law of Agency* (7th edition) by Fridman at pages 224–225).

If a third party, not knowing that a donee is in fact acting under a power of attorney, pays the donee, that will operate as a discharge for the third party, and the donor will not be able to sue the third party, even if the donee has not accounted to the donor for the money (*Coates and Another v Lewes and Another* (1808) 1 Camp 444, 170 ER 1015).

8. Election

A third party may have to elect whether to sue the donor or donee, as it would be clearly unjust to permit a third party to recover twice. In *Priestly v Fernie* (1865) 3 H & C 977, 159 ER 820, it was held that a third party could not sue the owner of a ship on a bill of lading having obtained judgment against the master of the ship who had signed the bill. Bramwell B at pages 983 and 984, 823 said:

> 'If this were an ordinary case of principal and agent, where the agent, having made a contract in his own name, has been sued on it to judgment, there can be no doubt that no second action would be maintainable against the principal.'

However, the mere issue of a writ will not usually amount to an election to sue that particular defendant, although the issue of a writ against either the donee or donor is a rebuttable presumption of an election (*Clarkson, Booker Ltd v Andjel* [1964] 3 All ER 260 at page 265). Therefore, a third party must elect whether to sue the donee or the donor, if both are liable, and having obtained judgment against one, an action cannot be brought against the other.

II. Enduring powers of attorney

1. Before the duty to register arises

A donee is under a duty to apply for registration of an enduring power in the event of the actual or impending mental incapacity of the donor (s 4 EPAA 1985; see Chapter 7). Until the duty to register arises, the power operates as an ordinary power, and the rights and liabilities of the donor and donee and third parties are the same whether the donee is acting under an ordinary power or an enduring power.

2. Between the duty to register arising and registration

During the period between the occurrence of the duty to register and registration, with some limited exceptions the donee may not do anything under the power (s 1(1)(b) EPAA 1985; see Chapter 7). It is submitted that transactions occurring during this period – and not subject to any of the exceptions – can be effective legally. Section 1(1)(c) EPAA 1985 applies s 5 Powers of Attorney Act 1971 to this situation. Section 5 is discussed in Chapter 12 in detail, but s 5(2) in effect provides that if a person deals with the donee of a power without knowledge of the mental incapacity, the transaction between them shall, in favour of that person, be as valid as if the power had then been in existence. It would thus seem that acts within the actual, implied, usual or ostensible authority of the donee of an enduring power between the duty to register arising and registration will have the same consequences as for ordinary powers, provided the third party is ignorant of the mental incapacity.

3. After registration

Section 7(1)(c) EPAA 1985 provides that the donor may not extend or restrict the scope of the authority conferred by the instrument, and no instruction or consent given by him after registration will, in the case of consent, confer any right and, in the case of an instruction, impose or confer any obligation or right on or create any liability of the attorney or other person having notice of the instruction or consent. The effect of this provision is that the authority of the donee is limited to the acts permitted by the power or the EPAA 1985; presumably this includes acts within the implied and usual authority of the donee, but not acts within the ostensible authority of the donee. However, it can be argued that any ostensible authority acquired by the donee before registration survives registration as s 7(1)(c) applies only to instructions or consents given after registration. Any act outside the authority of the attorney will not bind the donor, although the donee might be liable for breach of warranty of authority.

It should be noted that s 8(2)(f) EPAA 1985 authorises the court to relieve the attorney wholly or partly from any liability he has, or may have, incurred on account of a breach of his duties as an attorney.

Summary

- A donor is bound by all acts within the express authority of the donee.
- If the donee discloses the fact that he is an agent, the primary liability is that of the donor.
- There is some doubt as to whether a donor of a power of attorney can sue and be sued on a deed entered into by the donee.

- The donor will be bound by acts within the implied or usual authority of the donee.

- The donor will be bound by acts within the ostensible authority of the donee.

- The donor will be liable even if the donee fails to disclose the fact of agency.

- A third party may have to elect whether to sue the donor or donee if both are liable.

- If the donee is acting under an enduring power, rights and liabilities vary according to whether there is a duty to register, whether application has been made for registration, and whether the power has been registered.

Chapter 12

Protection of third parties and subsequent purchasers

Various events such as the death of the donor, cause the revocation of a power of attorney. Revocation is discussed fully in Chapter 6. If the power has been revoked, any transactions entered into by the donee will be void. This could cause serious injustice to a third party dealing with an attorney, who might have no means of finding out whether it had been revoked. To deal with this problem, both the Powers of Attorney Act 1971 and the Enduring Powers of Attorney Act 1985 ('EPAA 1985') contain provisions protecting third parties.

It is necessary to consider separately the protection afforded to persons dealing with the donee of an ordinary power and persons dealing with the donee of enduring powers.

I. Ordinary powers of attorney

1. Protection of persons dealing with the donee

Section 5(2) Powers of Attorney Act 1971 provides that where 'a power of attorney has been revoked and a person, without knowledge of the revocation, deals with the donee of the power, the transaction between them shall, in favour of that person, be as valid as if the power had then been in existence'.

If the attorney is acting within his *actual* authority, the person dealing with the attorney is clearly protected. It is submitted that this subsection also protects a person dealing with the attorney if the attorney is acting within his implied, usual or ostensible authority – these acts would have bound the donor if the power had then been in existence.

Thus a person dealing with an attorney without knowledge that the power had been revoked will be protected under s 5(2) Powers of Attorney Act 1971. What is meant by knowledge? Section 5(5) provides that knowledge of the revocation of a power of attorney includes knowledge of any event (such as the death of the donor) which has the effect of revoking the power. A person dealing with an attorney cannot argue that, although he knew about the death, he did not appreciate that that event revoked the power.

2. Protection of subsequent purchasers

Section 5(2) Powers of Attorney Act 1971 protects the person dealing with the donee of the power, and is not of much help to subsequent purchasers of the property as they may have difficulty in proving that the person dealing with the donee of a power of attorney did not have any knowledge of the revocation of the power. To assist subsequent purchasers, s 5(4) provides that where the interest of a purchaser depends on whether a transaction between the donee of a power of attorney and another person was valid by virtue of s 5(2), it will be conclusively presumed that the person dealing with the donee of the power did not at the material time know of the revocation of the power if:

(a) the transaction between that person and the donee was completed within twelve months of the date on which the power came into operation; or

(b) that person makes a statutory declaration, before or within three months after the completion of the purchase, that he did not at the material time know of the revocation of the power.

Example

A appoints B to be his attorney utilising the general power of attorney contained in Sch 1 Powers of Attorney Act 1971.

Two years later B sells A's house to C.

One year later C sells the house to D.

C is protected by s 5(2). D is not protected by s 5(4)(a) as the transaction between B and C was completed more than twelve months after the power came into operation. However, D is protected by s 5(4)(b) if C makes a statutory declaration before or within three months after the completion of the purchase by D that at the material time he did not know of the revocation of the power.

Section 5(5) should be borne in mind; this provides that knowledge of the revocation of a power of attorney includes knowledge of the occurrence of any event (such as the death of the donor) which has the effect of revoking the power.

Section 5(6) provides that 'purchaser' and 'purchase' have the meanings specified in s 205(1) Law of Property Act 1925. There 'purchaser' is defined as a purchaser in good faith for valuable consideration, and includes a lessee, mortgagee, or other person who for valuable consideration acquires an interest in property. So a purchaser from a person who dealt with an attorney (D in the example above) is not protected by s 5(4) if he was aware that the power had been revoked, but subsequent purchasers in good faith are protected.

3. Transferees under stock exchange transactions

Section 6(1) Powers of Attorney Act 1971 provides additional protection for transferees under stock exchange transactions. It provides that, without prejudice to s 5 of the Act, where:

(a) the donee of a power of attorney executes, as transferor, an instrument transferring registered securities; and

(b) the instrument is executed for the purpose of a stock exchange transaction,

it will be conclusively presumed in favour of the transferee that the power had not been revoked at the date of the instrument if a statutory declaration to that effect is made by the donee of the power on or within three months after that date.

4. Irrevocable powers

Section 4 Powers of Attorney Act 1971 deals with irrevocable powers given as security for a proprietary interest of the donee of the power, or for the performance of an obligation owed to the donee. The section provides that so long as the donee has that interest or the obligation remains undischarged, the power cannot be revoked by the donor without the consent of the donee; nor can it be revoked by the death, incapacity or bankruptcy of the donor or, if the donor is a body corporate, by its winding up or dissolution.

Where, in the instrument creating it, a power is expressed to be irrevocable and to be given by way of security then, unless the person dealing with the donee knows that it was not in fact given by way of security, s 5(3) provides that he will be entitled to assume that the power is incapable of revocation except by the donor acting with the consent of the donee; he will accordingly be treated for the purposes of s 5(2) as having knowledge of the revocation only if he knows that it has been revoked in that manner. Thus a person dealing with the donee of an irrevocable power will be protected unless he knows it has been revoked by the donor with the consent of the donee, or he knows the power was not given by way of security. Subsequent purchasers will be able to take advantage of the protection afforded by s 5(4).

Situations where a power can be made irrevocable:

(a)   A mortgagee may be given a power of attorney by the mortgagor to enable the mortgagee to sell the mortgaged property. Such a power is given both to secure a proprietary interest of the mortgagee or donee, and the performance of an obligation owed to the mortgagee or donee.

(b)   A partner may give his other partners a power of attorney limited to the affairs of the partnership. Such a power may secure a proprietary interest of the donee or partner; alternatively, or in addition, it may secure the obligations or duties owed by the donee of the power to the other partners.

(c)   In conveyancing transactions, builders sometimes take the existing house of a purchaser in part exchange for a new house. Rather than take a conveyance of the existing house, and incur liability for stamp duty, the builder is granted a power of attorney by the purchaser authorising the builder to transfer the purchaser's existing house to the purchaser from the builder. Such a power clearly secures a proprietary interest of the builder. Home relocation companies also take powers of attorney rather than a transfer of the house concerned.

5. Third party protection when power is void from the outset

It may be that a power is granted by someone who did not have the capacity to do so. A person dealing with the 'donee' of the power may have no means of ascertaining if this is the case, but any transaction under the power will be void (*Daily Telegraph Newspaper Co Ltd v McLaughlin* [1904] AC 777 and Chapter 9). The Powers of Attorney Act 1971 does not contain any provision protecting the attorney in this situation. However, an attorney lacking authority will be liable for breach of warranty of authority (see Chapter 11), and provided the attorney has enough money to satisfy any judgment, the third party will not suffer any loss. Accordingly, the risk in dealing with professionally qualified attorneys is slight. However, if a person dealing with an attorney suspects that all is not in order, further enquiries should be made as to the validity of the power.

II. Enduring powers of attorney

Section 5 Powers of Attorney Act 1971 protects persons dealing with the donee and subsequent purchasers. However, the EPAA 1985 has some additional provisions.

1. Protection of persons dealing with the donee

Section 1(2) EPAA 1985 applies to the period between application for registration of an enduring power, and the initial determination of that application. It permits the attorney to take action under the power to maintain the donor or prevent loss to his estate, or to maintain himself or other persons in so far as s 3(4) permits him to do so. Section 1(3) protects a person who deals with an attorney without knowledge that the attorney is acting outside s 1(2).

Section 9 EPAA 1985 deals with the situation where an instrument which did not create a valid power has been registered (whether or not the registration has been cancelled at the time of the act or transaction in question). For example, it applies to a power which was invalid because the donor lacked capacity at the time of the grant, but which had still been registered.

Section 9(3) EPAA 1985 provides that any transaction between the attorney and another person shall, in favour of that person, be as valid as if the power had then been in existence, unless at the time of the transaction that person knows that:

(a) the instrument did not create a valid enduring power; or

(b) an event has occurred which, if the instrument had created a valid enduring power, would have had the effect of revoking the power; or

(c) if the instrument had created a valid enduring power, the power would have expired before that time.

Schedule 2 EPAA 1985 provides further protection for a third person dealing with the donee of an invalid enduring power. It applies where an instrument framed in the prescribed form creates a power which is not a valid enduring power, and is revoked by the mental incapacity of the donor. Under Sch 2 para 3 any transaction between the attorney and another person shall, in favour of that person, be as valid as if the power had been in existence, unless at the time of the transaction that person knows that:

(a) the instrument did not create a valid power; and

(b) the donor has become mentally incapable.

2. Protection of subsequent purchasers

Section 9(3) and Sch 2 para 3 EPAA 1985 protect persons dealing with the attorney. Subsequent purchasers are protected by s 9(4) and Sch 2 para 4; these measures provide that where the interest of a purchaser depends on whether a transaction between the attorney and another person was valid by virtue of s 9(3) or Sch 2 para 3, it will be conclusively presumed in favour of the purchaser that the transaction was valid if:

(a) the transaction between that person and the attorney was completed within twelve months of the date on which the instrument was registered; or

(b) that person makes a statutory declaration, before or within three months after the completion of the purchase, that he had no reason at the time of the transaction to doubt that the attorney had authority to dispose of the property which was the subject of the transaction.

It will be recalled that s 9 applies to the situation where an instrument which did not create a valid power has been registered (whether or not the registration has been cancelled at the time of the act or transaction in question), and that Sch 2 applies to an instrument in the prescribed form which is not a valid enduring power, and which has been revoked by the mental incapacity of the donor.

Section 9(7) EPAA 1985 provides that 'purchaser' and 'purchase' have the meanings specified in s 205(1) Law of Property Act 1925. These are discussed above; if a purchaser is not acting in good faith, he will not be able to take advantage of s 9.

Section 9(5) EPAA 1985 states that if the donor revokes the power, and such revocation is invalid unless and until confirmed by the court, knowledge of the confirmation of the revocation is knowledge of the revocation. However, knowledge of the unconfirmed revocation does not amount to knowledge of the revocation of the power. Thus the donee of the power and any other person are not concerned with any revocation of the power until it has been confirmed by the court.

3. Applications of s 5 Powers of Attorney Act to enduring powers

Section 9(2) and (4) EPAA 1985 are of limited application – they apply only where an instrument which did not create a valid power has been registered. Schedule 2 applies where the instrument failed to create a valid enduring power, and the power has been revoked by the donor's mental incapacity (s 9(6)). In other situations, s 5 Powers of Attorney Act 1971 applies.

Although there are some limited exceptions, s 1(1)(b) EPAA 1985 provides that if the donor of an enduring power becomes mentally incapable, the donee of the power may not do anything under the authority of the power until it is registered. Section 1(1)(c) provides that s 5 Powers of Attorney Act 1971 applies to enduring powers for so long as the donor's authority is suspended under s 1(1)(b); this provision is necessary because s 5 applies only when the power has been revoked, and not merely suspended.

4. Third party protection when power is invalid

Section 9 and Sch 2 EPAA 1985 may be wide enough to protect the person dealing with the attorney under an invalid power. These are discussed above. A person who deals with a donee, or a purchaser from a donee, under a registered power which was invalid, or which is in the prescribed form but does not create a valid enduring power and is revoked by the mental incapacity of the donor, is in a much stronger position than a person who deals with a donee, or a purchaser from a donee, of an ordinary power.

Summary

- Section 5(2) Powers of Attorney Act 1971 protects a person dealing with an attorney without knowledge of the revocation of the power of attorney.
- Section 5(4) protects subsequent purchasers.
- Section 4 protects persons dealing with the donee of an irrevocable power.
- Section 9 EPAA 1985 provides additional protection for

persons dealing with the donees of invalid enduring powers which have been registered, and donees of powers in the prescribed form which are invalid and have been revoked by the mental incapacity of the donor.

- There is no protection for a person dealing with a 'donee' under an invalid ordinary power, but if it is an enduring power, such a person may be able to take advantage of s 9 EPAA 1985.

Chapter 13

Execution of documents, conveyancing and grants of representation

I. Execution of documents

1. By an individual

Section 7(1) Powers of Attorney Act 1971, as amended by the Law of Property (Miscellaneous Provisions) Act 1989, provides that the donee of a power of attorney may, if he thinks fit:

(a)   execute any instrument with his own signature, and

(b)   do any thing in his own name,

by the authority of the donor of the power; and any document executed or thing done in that manner is as effective as if executed or done by the donee with the signature and seal, or, as the case may be, in the name, of the donor of the power.

An attorney can thus execute a document using his own name or the name of the donor.

Section 74(3) Law of Property Act 1925 provides that where a person is authorised under a power of attorney to convey any interest in property in the name or on behalf of a company, he may as attorney execute the conveyance by signing the name of the company in the presence of at least one witness, and such execution takes effect and is valid as if the corporation had executed the conveyance.

Seciton 7(2) Powers of Attorney Act 1971 states that an instrument to which s 74(3) Law of Property Act 1925 applies may be executed either as provided in s 74(3) of the 1925 Act or as provided in s 7 of the 1971 Act.

2. By a company

If a company has been appointed an attorney, s 74(4) Law of Property Act 1925 provides that an officer appointed for that purpose by the board of directors by resolution, or otherwise, may execute the deed or other instrument in the name of such other person; and where an instrument appears to be so executed by an officer so appointed, then in favour of a purchaser the instrument will be deemed to have been executed by an officer duly authorised. Section 205(1)(xxi) defines a purchaser as meaning a purchaser in good faith for valuable consideration.

II. Conveyancing

1. Protection of purchasers

Section 5 Powers of Attorney Act 1971 and s 9 and Sch 2 EPAA 1985 protect purchasers dealing with the donee of both an ordinary and an enduring power. This topic is discussed in Chapter 12.

2. Registered conveyancing and powers of attorney

(a) Proof of powers of attorney

The Land Registration (Powers of Attorney) Rules 1986 (SI 1986 No 5137) substituted a new rule for r 82 Land Registration Rules 1925. The new r 82(1) provides that if an instrument executed by an attorney is delivered at the Registry, the registrar must be furnished with either;

(i) the instrument creating the power; or

(ii) a copy by means of which its contents may be proved under either s 3 Powers of Attorney Act 1971 or s 7(3) EPAA 1985 or a document which complies with s 4 Evidence and Powers of Attorney Act 1940.

Section 3(1) Powers of Attorney Act 1971 provides that the contents of an instrument creating a power of attorney may be proved by a copy which:

'(a) is a reproduction of the original made with a photographic or other device for reproducing documents in facsimile; and

(b) contains the following certificate or certificates signed by the donor of the power or by a solicitor or stockbroker, that is to say –

   (i) a certificate at the end to the effect that the copy is a true and complete copy of the original; and

   (ii) if the original consists of two or more pages, a certificate at the end of each page of the copy to the effect that it is a true and complete copy of the corresponding page of the original.'

Under s 3(2) the contents of an instrument creating a power of attorney may also be proved by a copy of a copy complying with s 3(1) if the further copy complies with s 3(1).

Section 3 applies to both ordinary powers and enduring powers. Section 7(3) EPAA 1985, which applies only to enduring powers, provides that a document purporting to be an office copy of an instrument registered under the EPAA 1985 will be evidence of the contents of the instrument and of the fact that it has been so registered. Section 7(4) EPAA 1985 provides that subs (3) is without prejudice to s 3 Powers of Attorney Act 1971 and to any other method of proof authorised by law.

Evidence of registration must also be supplied (see Practice Leaflet No 17 issued by the Land Registry).

Section 4 Evidence and Powers of Attorney Act 1940 is of little relevance today.

If it is an enduring power, and an order has been made under s 8 EPAA 1985, which deals with the functions of the court with respect to a registered power, the registrar must be supplied with a copy of the order or an office copy or copy certified pursuant to r 309 (r 82(2)). Rule 309 states that every copy of a document delivered by a solicitor at the Registry must be endorsed with his name and address and must be certified by him to be a true copy of the original. Such copy need not be stamped.

Under r 82(3) the registrar may retain any instrument creating a power of attorney, or any order, or any copy, or document produced pursuant to the rule.

(b) Proof of non-revocation of the power

If the transaction between the donee of the power of attorney and the person dealing with him is completed within twelve months of the date when the power came into force, the registrar will not usually require any additional evidence to the effect that the power has not been revoked. It will be recalled that s 5(2) Powers of Attorney Act 1971 provides that where a power of attorney has been revoked and a person, without knowledge of the revocation, deals with the donee of the power, the transaction between them shall, in favour of that person, be as valid as if the power had then been in existence. Section 5(4) provides that where the interest of a purchaser depends on whether a transaction between the donee of a power of attorney and another person was valid by virtue of subs (2), it will be conclusively presumed in favour of a purchaser that that person did not at the material time know of the revocation of the power if the transaction between that person was completed within twelve months of the date on which the power came into operation. The registrar is protected by both these provisions; in addition, any person who deals with the attorney, and who is aware that the power has been revoked, is not entitled to indemnity if the register is rectified against him (s 83(5)(a) Land Registration Act 1925; see paras 15–16 of *Registration of Title* by Ruoff and Roper).

If the transaction between the donee of the power of attorney and the person dealing with him is completed more than twelve months after the date on which the power came into operation, the registrar will require evidence that the power has not been revoked (r 82(4)). In the case of an enduring power of attorney, unless the registrar otherwise directs, this evidence must consist of a statutory declaration by the person dealing with the donee that he did not, at the time of the completion of the transaction:

   (i) know of any revocation of the power whether by the donor or by an Order of the Court of Protection;

  (ii) know of the occurrence of any event (such as the death of the donor or the bankruptcy of the donor or of any donee or a direction by the Court of Protection on exercising its powers under Pt VII Mental Health Act 1983) which had the effect of revoking the power;

 (iii) know that the power was not a valid enduring power of attorney and had been revoked by the donor's mental incapacity. (r 82(5)).

If the power of attorney is not in the form prescribed under s 2(2) EPAA 1985, unless the registrar otherwise directs, the evidence that the power has not been revoked must consist of a statutory declaration by the person dealing with the attorney that he did not, at the time of the completion of the transaction:

   (i) know of any revocation of the power; or

    (ii) know of the occurrence of any event (such as the death,
         bankruptcy or other incapacity of the donor) which had the
         effect of revoking the power.
         (r 82(6)).

By a Practice Direction of 26 April 1991, the Chief Land
Registrar has intimated that a certificate signed by a solicitor or
licensed conveyancer is acceptable instead of the statutory declaration which would otherwise have to be lodged with the Land
Registry. The certificate must contain the same statements as
would have to be contained in the statutory declarations.
However, if the instrument which created the power expressed it
to be irrevocable and to be given by way of security, the statutory declaration must be to the effect that the declarant did not
know that the power was not in fact given by way of security
and did not know that the power had been revoked by the donor
acting with the consent of the donee.

3. Joint tenants and tenants in common

This topic is discussed in Chapter 9.

III. Grants of representation to an attorney

1. Effect of mental incapacity on existing grants

If a sole executor or administrator, or the sole surviving executor
or administrator, appoints an attorney under an enduring power,
and then becomes mentally incapable, the attorney cannot continue
with the administration of the estate, even if the power has been
registered.

Similarly, if one of two or more executors or administrators
becomes mentally incapable having appointed an attorney under an
enduring power, the attorney cannot take over the administration of
the estate. (See Practice Direction [1986] 2 All ER 41.)

2. Procedure on an application by an attorney

If a donor of an enduring or ordinary power of attorney is entitled
to apply for a grant of probate or letters of administration, his attorney can apply for administration for the use and benefit of the
donor under r 31(1) Non-Contentious Probate Rules 1987 (SI 1987

No 2024), provided he has authority to do so under the power; a general power gives such authority. The grant may be limited until further representation be granted, or in such other way as the registrar may direct.

If an attorney is applying on behalf of a donor who is an executor, notice of the application must be given to any other executor unless such notice is dispensed with by the registrar (r 31(2)), but the rules do not require an attorney acting on behalf of a donor who is entitled to a grant of letters of administration to give notice to other persons who are equally entitled to apply for a grant of letters of administration.

If the donor was appointed an executor, the attorney will be given a grant of letters of administration with the will annexed. The donor of the power, or if more than one executor was appointed, another executor, can apply for a grant of probate, and if that grant is made, the grant of letters of administration with the will annexed will terminate.

Even if there is a grant to an attorney, it will still be necessary to comply with s 114(2) Supreme Court Act 1981. This provides that where under a will or intestacy, any beneficiary is a minor, or a life interest arises, any grant of administration by the High Court must be made either to a trust corporation (with or without an individual) or to no fewer than two individuals unless it appears to the court to be expedient in all the circumstances to appoint an individual as sole administrator.

An attorney applying for a grant should lodge with the Probate Registry the instrument creating the power of attorney, or alternatively a copy certified in accordane with s 3 Powers of Attorney Act 1971.

If the donor is mentally incapable, and the attorney is acting under an enduring power, r 31(3) requires the application to be made in accordance with r 35. Rule 35(1) provides that, unless the registrar otherwise directs, no grant will be made under the rule unless all the persons entitled in the same degree as the donor have been cleared off. Rule 22(1) lays down the order of priority for a grant of letters of administration; if there is anyone in the same class as the donor, r 35 does not apply until all the persons in that class have been cleared off.

Rule 35(2) provides that where a registrar is satisfied that a person entitled to a grant is by reason of mental incapacity incapable of managing his own affairs, administration for his use and benefit, limited until further representation be granted or in such other way as the registrar may direct, may be granted in the following order of priority:

- to the person authorised by the Public Trust Office to apply for a grant;
- where there is no person so authorised, to the lawful attorney of the incapable person acting under a registered enduring power of attorney;
- where there is no such attorney entitled to act, or if the attorney renounces administration for the use and benefit of the incapable person, to the person entitled to the residuary estate of the deceased.

If the enduring power is registered, no further proof of mental incapacity is required.

If it is a situation where two administrators are required because either a beneficiary is a minor or a life interest arises, and if there is only one person competent and willing to take a grant under the rule, administration may be granted to such person jointly with any other person nominated by him, unless a registrar otherwise directs (r 35(3)).

Under r 35(5), notice of an intended application under this rule must be given to the Public Trust Office.

For a fuller discussion of these matters readers are referred to *Butterworth's Wills, Probate and Administration Service*, division D.

Summary

- The donee of a power of attorney can execute a document in his own name.
- The existence or terms of a power of attorney can be proved by the production of the original or a certified copy, or if it is an enduring power which has been registered, an office copy.
- If an order has been made under s 8 EPAA 1985, if the title is registered, the registrar must be supplied with a copy of the order, or an office copy or a certified copy.
- If the transaction between the donee of the power of attorney and the person dealing with him is completed more than twelve months after the date on which the power came into operation, the person dealing with the donee will have to make a statutory declaration. A certificate may be accepted.

- The donee of an ordinary or enduring power may have authority to take out a grant of probate or letters of administration if the donee would have been entitled to do so.

Chapter 14

Procedure in the Court of Protection

It may be that a person becomes mentally incapable without having executed an enduring power of attorney. In these circumstances, if it is desired to deal with the property of that person, it will be necessary to apply to the Court of Protection.

1. Extent of the powers of the Court of Protection

Section 95(1) Mental Health Act 1983 provides that the judge may, with respect to the property and affairs of a patient, do or secure the doing of all such things as appear necessary or expedient:

(a) for the maintenance or other benefit of the patient,

(b) for the maintenance or other benefit of members of the patient's family,

(c) for making provision for other persons or purposes for whom or which the patient might be expected to provide if he were not mentally disordered, or

(d) otherwise for administering the patient's affairs.

'Family' in s 95(1)(b) means persons for all of whom the patient might *prima facie* be expected to make some provision, and does not include collateral relatives such as nephews and nieces. Such people must bring themselves within s 95(1)(c) as persons for whom the patient might be expected to provide if he were not mentally disordered (per Cross J in *Re DML* [1965] 2 All ER 129 at pages 131–132).

Section 96(1) confers wide powers on the judge to make orders or give directions or authorities for:

(a) the control (with or without the transfer or vesting of property or the payment into or lodgement in the Supreme Court of money or securities) and the management of any property of the patient;

(b) the sale, exchange, charging or other disposition of or dealing with any property of the patient;

(c) the acquisition of any property in the name or on behalf of the patient;

(d) the settlement of any property of the patient, or the gift of any property of the patient to any such persons or for any such purposes as are mentioned in paragraph (b) and (c) of s 95(1) above;

(e) the execution for the patient of a will making any provision (whether by way of disposing of property or exercising a power or otherwise) which could be made by a will executed by the patient if he were not mentally disordered;

(f) the carrying on by a suitable person of any profession, trade or business of the patient;

(g) the dissolution of a partnership of which the patient is a member;

(h) the carrying out of any contract entered into by the patient;

(i) the conduct of legal proceedings in the name of the patient or on his behalf;

(j) the reimbursement out of the property of the patient, with or without interest, of money applied by any person either in payment of the patient debtors's debts (whether legally enforceable or not) or for the maintenance or other benefit of the patient or members of his family or in making provision for other persons or purposes for whom or which he might be expected to provide if he were not mentally disordered;

(k) the exercise of any power (including a power to consent) vested in the patient whether beneficially, or as guardian or trustee, or otherwise.

How will the court exercise its powers? In *Re C* [1960] 1 All ER 393 a receiver had been appointed for a patient, and then discharged. The patient had then dissipated quite a large sum of money. A receiver had then been appointed, and it was proposed to make an irrevocable settlement of his property. This was authorised under broadly similar powers in the Law of Property Act 1925 to those contained in the Mental Health Act 1983. Danckwerts J, at page 396, said: 'This is a case where it is proper and desirable that the court should restrain the patient if he comes out into the world again, so that he is not able to squander his property to his own detriment.'

In *M v Lester* [1966] 1 All ER 207 the infant plaintiff suffered brain damage, and was awarded damages of £15,000. It was directed that the money should be invested under the supervision of the Court of Protection, and that application for the appointment of a receiver should be made.

A settlement can also be ordered even if it will result in a saving of tax (*Re CWM* [1951] 2 All ER 707).

Section 96(3) provides that if a settlement has been made, it can be varied if:

(a) a material fact was not disclosed when the settlement was made; or

(b) there has been a substantial change in circumstances.

This power to vary can only be exercised whilst the patient is alive.

The procedure in the Court of Protection is governed by the Court of Protection Rules 1994, SI 1994 No 3046 ('CPR 1994'). Readers are warned not to confuse these rules with SI 1994 No 3047, which is concerned with the registration of enduring powers of attorney.

2. When can an application be made for the appointment of a receiver?

The court can appoint a receiver if a person is incapable, by reason of mental disorder, of managing and administering his property and affairs (s 94 Mental Health Act 1983). Section 1(2) Mental Health Act 1983 defines mental disorder as meaning mental illness, arrested or incomplete development of mind, psychopathic disorder and any other disorder or disability of mind.

3. Functions of the Public Trustee

Rule 6 CPR 1994 authorises the Public Trustee to exercise all the functions conferred on the judge by Part VII of the Act. However, the following functions can only be exercised by the court:

(a) the resolution of any contested application including any interim matters relating to it;

(b) the appointment and discharge of a receiver under s 99 of the 1983 Act;

(c) the appointment of a new receiver;

(d) the appointment of an interim receiver under r 44 CPR 1994;

(e) subject to r 9 CPR 1994, the determination of jurisdiction of the court under s 94(2) of the 1983 Act;

(f) the making of orders on applications under ss 96(1)(e), (i) and (k), 98, 100, 103 and 104 of the 1983 Act (s 100 deals with the vesting of stock in a curator appointed outside England and Wales; s 103 deals with visitors (see also pages 155–156); s 104 deals with the general powers of the judge with respect to proceedings);

(g) the making of orders under s 96(1)(d) or 96(2) of the 1983 Act except where, in respect of a gift, it is payable out of the surplus income or capital, is insignificant in the context of the patient's assets and is for a sum which is not more than £15,000;

(h) the making of orders relating to loans or other financial transactions where there is an element of gift except where it is payable out of the surplus income or capital, is insignificant in the context of the patient's assets and is for a sum which is not more than £15,000;

(i) the making of directions under s 101 of the 1983 Act and in respect of property to which s 101 applies and for the severance of joint tenancies (s 101 is concerned with the preservation of interests in patient's property);

(j) the making of directions relating to any assets of a patient that are the subject of specific bequests or devises in his will;

(k) the making of orders under s 36(9) or 54 Trustee Act 1925 (s 36 is concerned with the appointment of new trustees; s 54 deals with the powers of the Court of Protection when a patient is also a trustee);

(l) the making of orders determining the proceedings;

(m) the making of orders relating to assets situated outside England and Wales and for the transfer of assets out of England and Wales;

(n) the giving of such directions as may be appropriate in relation to a will made or proposed to be made by a patient.

Rule 6(3) CPR 1994 permits the Public Trustee to refer any matter to the court for determination.

If the Public Trustee is appointed a receiver, he may do anything which he is empowered to authorise a receiver to do.

Rule 12 CPR 1994 provides that where in the opinion of the court an application ought to be made for the appointment or discharge of a receiver or for the exercise of any other function with respect to the property and affairs of a patient, and there appears to be no other suitable person able and willing to make the application, or the court for any other reason thinks fit, the court may direct that the application be made by the Public Trustee or, if he consents, by the Official Solicitor.

Rule 13 CPR 1994 provides that where it appears to the Public Trustee that an application should be made to the court for the exercise of any of its functions or that any of his own functions ought to be exercised, he may make an application or exercise such functions of his own motion.

4. Exercise of jurisdiction of the court

Rule 7 CPR 1994 gives the court a wide discretion as to how the jurisdiction is exercised. It provides that, except where the rules otherwise provide, the jurisdiction of the court may be exercised:

(a)   without fixing an appointment for a hearing;

(b)   by the court or the Public Trustee as appropriate of its own motion or at the instance or on the application of any person interested;

(c)   whether or not any proceedings have been commenced in the court with respect to the patient.

5. Form of application

Rule 8 CPR 1994 provides that a first application to the court for the appointment of a receiver must be in Form CP1. An application to the court respecting the exercise of any of its other jurisdiction in relation to a patient may be by letter unless the court directs that formal application must be made. In this situation, Form B must be used.

Rule 8(2) CPR 1994 deals with applications to the Public Trustee for the exercise of any of his functions. Such applications are to be made by letter or in such manner as he shall direct. He can direct that Form B should be used for applications.

If the application is urgent, the court may dispense with the need for an application in writing (r 8(4)).

Rule 36(1) CPR 1994 provides that on the issue of a first application for the appointment of a receiver for a patient, or for an order authorising any person to do any act or carry out any transaction on behalf of a patient without appointing him a receiver, the applicant must file a medical certificate and evidence of family and property, unless the court otherwise directs.

A medical certificate is defined as a certificate by a medical practitioner that the patient is incapable, by reason of mental disorder, of managing and administering his property and affairs. Evidence of family and property means a certificate or, if the court so orders in a particular case, an affidavit, giving particulars of the patient's relatives, property and affairs and of the circumstances giving rise to the application. The relevant forms are CP3(PT) and CP5(PT).

Upon receipt of an application under r 8, the court fixes a date for the hearing of the application. However, it need not do so if it considers that the application can properly be dealt with without a hearing – and once a hearing date has been fixed, it can be cancelled on the same grounds (r 10).

It may be that application is made in respect of a husband and wife, or brothers and sisters. Rule 11 provides that the court may allow one application to be made in respect of two or more patients or may consolidate applications relating to two or more patients, if in the opinion of the court the proceedings relating to them can be more conveniently dealt with together.

The court or the Public Trustee may allow or direct an applicant to amend his application. The amendment may be effected by making in writing the necessary alterations to the application, but if the amendments are so numerous or of such a nature or length that written alterations would be difficult or inconvenient to read, a fresh application amended as authorised or direction may be issued (r 53).

There is also provision for a short order or direction without the appointment of a receiver where it appears to the court that the property of the patient does not exceed £5,000 in value, or it is otherwise appropriate to proceed under this rule, and that it is not necessary to appoint a receiver (r 9(2)). Rule 9(3) **CPR 1994** provides that an order under this rule is an order directing an officer of the court or some other suitable person named in the order to deal with the patient's property, or any part, or with his affairs, in any manner authorised by the Act and specified in the order.

It is appropriate to use the direction procedure when the estate comprises cash, or premium savings bonds, national savings certificates and national savings income bonds. It is not appropriate if the patient has investment income, or is interested under a trust, or has a pension where the gross income exceeds £1,200 per annum (see *Making an Application*, the booklet published by the Public Trust Office).

Application for a direction is by submitting forms CP1(PT), CP3(PT) and CP5(PT).

6. Service of notice of the hearing

Rule 21 CPR 1994 provides that an applicant must give notice of the hearing of an application to:

(a)   the receiver for a patient, unless he is the applicant; and

(b)   such other persons as appear to the court to be interested and as the court may specify.

If the application is under s 54 Trustee Act 1925, which applies when the patient is also a trustee, or under s 96(1)(k) which is concerned with the exercise of any power vested in the patient whether beneficially or as guardian or trustee or otherwise, r 21(3) provides that notice of hearing must also be given to every person who, according to the practice of the Chancery Division, would have been required to be served with the summons if the application had been made to the High Court.

In the case of a first application for the appointment of a receiver, r 21(5) provides that notice of the hearing of an application must be given not less than ten clear days before the date fixed for the hearing. In the case of any other application, notice must be given at least two clear days before. Rule 21(6) provides that notice of a hearing is given if a copy of the sealed application is served on the person concerned.

The normal mode of service is personal delivery on the person to be served. If the court so directs, however, notice can be served by sending it to the last known address of the person required to be served (r 22). Under r 23 a solicitor acting for the person to be served can accept service on behalf of that person by endorsing on the document or a copy of it a statement to the effect that he accepts service on behalf of that person. If it is impracticable to serve any document in accordance with r 22, the court may make an order for substituted service of the document by taking such steps as the court may direct to bring it to the notice of the person to be served. Normally personal service of a first application for the appointment of a receiver is required.

Rule 25 provides that any document required to be served on a person who is a minor but is not also a patient must be served on his parent or guardian or, if he has no parent or guardian, on the person with whom he resides or in whose care he is.

In the case of a patient, the document must be served:

(a) on his receiver; or, if he has no receiver,

(b) on the person acting in pursuance of an order or direction made under r 9; or, if there is no such person,

(c) on an attorney acting under a registered power of attorney; or, if there is no such attorney,

(d) on the person with whom he resides or in whose care he is.

Under r 25(2) the court has power to order that a document has been duly served on such a person.

Rule 28(1) CPR 1994 provides that a certificate of service showing where, when, how and by whom service was effected must be filed as soon as practicable after service of a document has been effected in accordance with these rules.

7. Notification of application for the appointment of a receiver

Rule 26(1) provides that the patient must be notified in such manner as the court may direct where:

(a) a first application is made for the appointment of a receiver for a patient or for an order authorising a person to do any act or carry out any transaction on behalf of a patient without appointing him a receiver; or

(b) the court proposes to make a short order or the Public Trustee proposes to give a direction with respect to a patient's property under r 9 (short procedure).

Rule 26(2) provides that the court – or, where r 9(1)(b) applies, the Public Trustee – may at any time direct that no such notification shall be given if it is satisfied that:

(a) the patient is incapable of understanding it; or

(b) such notification would be injurious to the patient's health; or

(c) for any other reason notification ought to be dispensed with.

Where the patient is a minor, notification must be given to his parent or guardian or, if he has no parent or guardian, to the person with whom he resides or in whose care he is, unless the court otherwise directs (r 26(4)).

Next of kin may also have to be notified of the application. Rule 27(1) provides that where an applicant proposes to make an application for the appointment of a receiver or a new receiver, the applicant must give notice of his intention to:

(a)   all relatives of the patient who have the same or a nearer degree of relationship to the patient than the applicant or proposed receiver; and

(b)   such other persons as the court may specify who appear to the court to be interested.

The court can direct that such notification be dispensed with.

Rule 27(2) CPR 1994 provides that for the purposes of the rule, notice of intention to make an application is given if the person concerned is notified by letter of the identities of the patient, the applicant and the proposed receiver and what the application is for.

Rule 21(5) provides that notice of the hearing must be given not less than ten clear days before the date fixed for the hearing.

8. Representation of the patient

Rule 14(1) CPR 1994 provides that if a receiver has been appointed, any application on behalf of the patient must be made by the receiver in his own name. Rule 14(2) provides that subject to any directions given by the court, a patient for whom a receiver has been appointed may be represented by the receiver at any hearing relating to the patient or of which the patient has been given notice.

It may be that the interests of the patient cannot be adequately represented by the receiver. In this situation, the court may direct that the Official Solicitor shall act as solicitor if he consents.

9. Urgent applications

Section 98 Mental Health Act 1983 provides that where it is represented to the judge, and he has reason to believe, that a person may be incapable, by reason of mental disorder, of managing and administering his property and affairs, and the judge is of the opinion that it is necessary to make immediate provision for any of the matters referred to in s 95 (see page 142), then pending the determination of the question whether that person is so incapable, the judge may exercise in relation to the property and affairs of that person any of the powers conferred on him in relation to the property and affairs of a patient.

If the application is urgent, the court or the Public Trustee may dispense with the need for an application in writing (r 8(4)). This appears to apply to applications whether under rule 8(1) or rule 8(2) or rule 8(3).

10. Evidence

Rule 29 CPR 1994 provides that except where the rules otherwise provide, evidence in proceedings under the rules shall be given by affidavit evidence. Rule 30(1) provides that the court may accept and act upon a statement of facts or such other evidence, whether oral or written, as the court considers sufficient, although not given on oath. It does not matter that the evidence would not be admissible in a court of law apart from this rule. Rule 30(2) provides that the court may give directions as to the manner in which a statement of facts or other written evidence is to be given but, subject to such directions, any such statement or other evidence must be:

(a)   drawn up in numbered paragraphs and dated; and

(b)   signed by the person by whom it is made or given.

Rule 32 provides that any person who has made an affidavit, or given a certificate or other written evidence for use in proceedings, may be ordered by the court to attend for cross-examination.

Normally any affidavit, certificate or other written evidence must be filed in the court before it can be used in any proceedings under the rules. However, the court may make an order on the basis of such evidence before it is filed if the person tendering it undertakes to file it before the order is drawn up (r 34). Rule 34(2) provides that every affidavit, certificate or other written evidence must be endorsed with the name and address of the solicitor, if any, for the person on whose behalf it is filed.

Rule 35 provides that evidence used in any proceedings can be used in a subsequent stage of those proceedings or in any other proceedings relating to the same patient or to another member of the patient's family.

Rule 50(1) provides that the court may allow or direct any party or the Official Solicitor to take out a witness summons in Form C requiring the person named therein to attend before the court and give oral evidence or produce any document. Rule 50(3) provides that a witness summons must be served personally on the witness. Service must be a reasonable time before the day fixed for attendance, and the witness is entitled to the same conduct money and payment for expenses and loss of time as if he had been summoned to attend the trial of an action in the High Court.

Rule 52 authorises the judge or Master to make an order for the patient's attendance at such time and place as he may direct for examination by the Master, a visitor or any medical practitioner. See also pages 155–156 below.

11. Hearing of proceedings

Rule 39 CPR 1994 provides that every application shall be heard in chambers unless, in the case of an application for hearing by a judge, the judge otherwise directs. Rule 40 provides that the court may determine which persons should be entitled to attend at any stage of the proceedings relating to the patient.

Usually the application will be endorsed on issue 'Attendance not required unless notified'.

Rule 41 provides that if two or more persons are represented by the same legal adviser, the court may require them to be separately represented. Rule 42 applies when the function of the court is not being exercised by a judge, and requires the court to refer to the judge any proceedings or any question arising in any proceedings which ought by virtue of any enactment or in the opinion of the Master to be considered by the judge. The Master can give such directions as he thinks fit. Rule 43 authorises the judge to refer any proceedings before him or any question arising therein to the Master for inquiry and report.

12. Receivers

Rule 44 CPR 1994 authorises the court or the Public Trustee to make immediate provision in relation to the property and affairs of a patient. This can be done by a certificate directing or authorising any person named therein to do any act or carry out any transaction specified in the certificate. Alternatively, the court can appoint an interim receiver for the patient. Subject to any directions given by the court, such appointment continues until further order.

An order appointing an interim receiver shall, unless the court otherwise directs, be served upon the patient within such time as the court may specify. The patient may, within such time as the order may specify, apply under r 56 for the reconsideration of the order by the court or, if the order was made by a judge, apply to have the order set aside.

Usually a draft order will be prepared and sent to the solicitor for the applicant for approval.

Rule 45 authorises the court to allow the receiver remuneration for his services at such amount or at such rate as the court considers reasonable and proper. Any remuneration so allowed constitutes a debt due to the receiver from the patient and his estate. Once a patient has died, it is not possible to ask for remuneration, unless the court has during the receivership directed that remuneration shall be allowed, and the request is made within six years from the date of the discharge of the receiver.

It is possible for two or more persons to be appointed receivers, and the court can direct that the receivership should continue in favour of the surviving or continuing receiver(s).

Rule 48(1) provides that where:

(a) an order is made on a first application appointing a receiver for a patient or directing or authorising any person to do any act or carry out any transaction on behalf of a patient without appointing him a receiver, or

(b) an order or direction with respect to a patient's property is made under r 9 (short procedure – see page 147),

the order or direction is not to be entered until the expiration of ten clear days after the patient has been notified of the application. This means that the order or direction will not be effective until ten days after the patient has been notified of the application. This rule does not apply to any order for interim provision under r 44.

13. Security

Rule 58 CPR 1994 requires a receiver to give security for the due performance of his duties, and this security must be given before the receiver acts, unless the court allows it to be given subsequently. This obligation does not apply if the Public Trustee or Official Solicitor is appointed as receiver. Rule 59 provides that subject to any directions of the court, security may be given in any of the following ways, or a combination of such ways:

(a) by a bond approved by the court and given by the person giving security and also by –

  (i) an insurance company, group of underwriters, or bank approved by the Public Trustee; or

  (ii) two personal sureties approved by the Public Trustee; or

(b) by lodging in the court a sufficient sum of money or stock; or

(c) in such other manner as the Public Trustee may approve.

Rule 60 provides that any security given by lodgement of money or stock shall be dealt with in accordance with the terms of the direction filed when the lodgement was made.

Rule 62 provides that every person who has given security by a bond shall, whenever his accounts are passed or the Public Trustee so directs, satisfy the court:

(a) that any premiums payable in respect of the bond have been duly paid, or

(b) if the bond was given by personal sureties, that each surety is living and within the jurisdiction and has neither been adjudicated bankrupt nor compounded with his creditors.

If the Public Trustee is not so satisfied, he may require new security to be given or may give such other direction as he thinks fit.

Rule 61 provides that where a receiver is authorised or directed to give new security, and:

(a) the new security has been completed, and

(b) he has paid or secured to the satisfaction of the Public Trustee any balance due from him,

the former security shall be discharged, unless the Public Trustee otherwise directs.

14. Investments

The court has developed investment policies which are set out in Factsheet 3 issued by the Court of Protection. The investments which will be permitted depend *inter alia* on the period for which investment is required, and the amount of money involved.

15. Accounts

It is clearly essential for a receiver to keep accounts. Rule 63(1) CPR 1994 obliges every receiver annually or at such other times as the Public Trustee may direct to deliver his accounts to the Public Trustee and attend at or within such time as the Public Trustee may appoint to have the accounts taken and passed. Rule 63(3) provides that on the passing of any accounts, the Public Trustee shall make proper allowance out of the patient's estate, including an allowance in respect of the reasonable and proper costs of the receiver of passing the accounts and of any other person allowed to attend. Rule 63(4) provides that the court or the Public Trustee may, if it thinks fit, direct that a receiver need not account under this rule or may dispense with the passing of any accounts at any time at which they would otherwise require to be passed. Instead, there may be an annual enquiry when the receiver will be asked to respond to various questions about the financial affairs of the patient, but will not be required to produce annual accounts. This procedure is used if the receiver is the spouse of the patient, or lives in the same household, or is employed by the local authority (see Factsheets 1 and 2 issued by the Court of Protection).

If any money is due from the receiver, it should be paid into court to the credit of the proceedings and invested in such manner as the Public Trustee may direct, or be invested or otherwise dealt with by the receiver in such manner as the Public Trustee may direct (r 64).

If the receiver defaults in these obligations, the court or the Public Trustee may disallow any remuneration which would otherwise be due to the receiver. If the receiver has defaulted in paying into court or investing or otherwise dealing with any money, he may be charged interest at such rate as the court may determine for the period of his default (r 65).

Rule 66 provides that unless otherwise directed, any money ordered to be paid by a receiver for maintenance shall be paid out of income, and any costs ordered to be paid by a receiver may, when taxed or fixed, be paid out of any monies coming into his hands, after providing for any maintenance and fees payable under these rules.

Rule 67(1) provides that when a receivership terminates, the Public Trustee shall take and pass the accounts of the receiver from the foot of his last account or, if no account of his has previously been passed, from the date of his appointment, unless in the opinion of the Public Trustee the taking and passing of such accounts may properly be dispensed with. Rule 67(2) provides that if a balance is found due from the receiver or his estate, he or his personal representatives, as the case may be, must pay it into court or otherwise deal with it as the Public Trustee may direct. On the other hand, if a balance is found to be due to the receiver or his estate, it must be paid to him or his personal representatives, as the case may be, by the patient or out of the patient's estate (r 67(3)). Rule 67(4) provides that on the payment of any balance due from the receiver, or if no balance is found due from him or the passing of his accounts has been dispensed with, the security of the receiver shall, unless the court otherwise directs, be discharged.

16. Inquiries

Section 102 Mental Health Act 1983 provides for three panels of visitors: medical, legal and general. Members are appointed by the Lord Chancellor, and medical visitors must be registered medical practitioners who appear to the Lord Chancellor to have special knowledge and experience of cases of mental disorder. Legal visitors must be barristers or solicitors of not less than ten years' standing.

Visitors may interview the patient in private, and a medical visitor may carry out in private a medical examination of the patient, and may require the production of and inspect any medical records relating to the patient.

Rule 69(1) provides that where a court has reason to believe that a receiver should be appointed for a patient or that any other power conferred on the court should be exercised with respect to the property and affairs of the patient, the court may direct:

(a)   a medical or legal visitor, the Public Trustee or, if he consents, the Official Solicitor, or any other appropriate person to visit the patient and report to the court whether it is desirable in the interests of the patient that an application should be made for that purpose, and in the case of a report by a medical or legal visitor, whether there is any other matter which the court should consider before exercising its functions in relation to a patient's property and affairs; or

(b)   a medical visitor to visit the patient and report to the court on the capacity of the patient to manage and administer his property and affairs.

On receiving any such report, the court may, if it thinks fit:

(a)   direct an application to be made pursuant to r 12 (see pages 145–146); or

(b)   if the report is by a medical visitor and the court is satisfied that the patient is incapable, by reason of mental disorder, of managing and administering his property and affairs, make an order appointing a receiver or exercising any other power conferred on the court with respect to the patient's property and affairs.

The court may inspect the property of the patient, or direct an officer of the court or, if he consents, the Official Solicitor, the Public Trustee or any other appropriate person to inspect the property, make any necessary inquiries and report to the court (r 70).

Rule 71 empowers the court to make or cause to be made such inquiries as it thinks fit as to any dealings with the patient's property before the commencement of the proceedings and as to the mental capacity of the patient at the time of such dealing. The court can also make inquiries as to whether the patient has executed any testamentary document, and make what other inquiries it considers necessary or expedient for the proper discharge of its functions under the Mental Health Act or the Court of Protection Rules (rr 72 and 73).

17. Custody and disposal of funds and other property

Rule 74 CPR 1994 deals with the situation where any furniture or effects of a patient are allowed by the court to remain in the possession of, or are deposited with, any person. That person must sign and file a statement of the furniture or effects and an undertaking not to part with them except on a direction under seal.

Rule 75 empowers the court to order some proper person to transfer stock in the name of the patient or receiver to the receiver, a new receiver, or into court.

What happens if a patient dies or recovers? Rule 76(1) provides that on the death or recovery of a patient the court may order any money, securities or other property belonging to the patient, or forming part of his estate, or remaining under the control of or held under the directions of the court, to be paid, transferred, delivered or released to the person who appears to be entitled thereto. If the patient dies, and his estate is less than £5,000 after allowing for the debts and funeral expenses, the Public Trustee may if it thinks fit provide for the payment of the funeral expenses, and then order that the balance should be transferred either to the personal representatives of the deceased or to the person who appears to be entitled to apply for a grant of representation (r 76(3)).

18. Sale of land

It may be necessary to sell the house in which the patient lived. For example, it may be that the patient is living with relatives, or is in hospital, and the patient's house has not been lived in for some time. If the sale has not already been authorised by the court, it is necessary to apply to the Public Trustee for a direction permitting the sale. Once a purchaser has been found a certificate of value must be lodged; in some circumstances, for example if the receiver is purchasing the property, an affidavit of value will have to be filed. There is no need to submit the contract or transfer to the court for approval.

After completion, the solicitor for the receiver must submit a completion statement to the Public Trust office. The balance of the purchase price is to be placed on deposit.

(See PN8 issued by the Court of Protection.)

19. Co-ownership

Frequently the house will be vested in the name of the patient and the patient's spouse as trustees holding on trust for themselves as joint tenants or tenants in common. Section 36(1) Trustee Act 1925 provides that where a trustee is unfit to act or is incapable of acting, then:

(a) the person(s) nominated for the purpose of appointing new trustees by the instrument creating the trust; or

(b) if there is no such person, or no such person able and willing to act, then the surviving or continuing trustee(s) for the time being, or the personal representatives of the last surviving or continuing trustee,

may by writing appoint one or more other persons (whether or not the person exercising the power) to be a trustee or trustees in the place of the unfit or incapable trustee.

The number of trustees must not be increased beyond four (s 34(2)).

Section 36(9) Trustee Act 1925 provides that where a trustee is incapable, by reason of mental disorder within the meaning of the Mental Health Act 1983, of exercising his functions as trustee and is also entitled in possession to some beneficial interest in the trust property, he may not be replaced as trustee without the leave of the Court of Protection. If a receiver has been appointed, then application can be by letter to the court.

Section 41 Trustee Act 1925 empowers the court to appoint new trustees; it is specifically authorised to do so if a trustee is incapable of exercising his functions as a trustee by reason of mental disorder within the meaning of the Mental Health Act 1983.

Rule 18 provides that no person other than a co-trustee, or other person with power to appoint a new trustee, may make an application to the court under s 36(9) Trustee Act 1925 for leave to appoint a new trustee in place of a patient.

Section 54(2) Trustee Act 1925 applies *inter alia* where a patient is a trustee under an express, implied or constructive trust, and is also beneficially entitled, for example where spouses are co-owners. If a receiver appointed by the Court of Protection is acting for him, or an application for the appointment of a receiver has been made but not determined, the Court of Protection has concurrent jurisdiction with the High Court in relation to the trust property. This does not apply to a trust which is subject to an order for administration made by the High Court.

Rule 17 CPR 1994 provides that an application to the court under s 54(2) may be made only by:

(a)   the receiver for the patient; or

(b)   any person who has made an application for the appointment of a receiver which has not yet been determined; or

(c)   a continuing trustee; or

(d)   any other person who, according to the practice of the Chancery Division, would have been entitled to make the application if it had been made to the High Court.

Rule 21(3) provides that notice of hearing must also be given to every person who, according to the practice of the Chancery Division, would have been required to be served with the summons if the application had been made to the High Court.

(See PN4 issued by the Court of Protection.)

20. Can the receiver benefit persons other than the patient?

The provisions of s 95 Mental Health Act 1983 are set out at the beginning of this chapter.

In *Re WJGL* [1965] 3 All ER 865 the court was concerned with a similar provision in the Mental Health Act 1959. The question was whether the court should authorise a lifetime settlement, and it was held that it should. Cross J said at pages 871–872:

'It seems to me ... that I must assume that the patient becomes a sane man for a sufficient time to review the situation but knows that after a brief interval of sanity he will once more be as he was before. On that footing he would see himself a bachelor of sixty-eight who will never marry or have a family.... He would know that he will never have any friends, other than H.J.S. and the receiver, or any interests.'

The judge made further assumptions, and then continued:

'Making those very curious assumptions I have no doubt that the patient would execute an irrevocable settlement of a substantial part of his property; on the other hand, I do not think that it follows from those assumptions that he would leave himself no more than he could foresee that he was likely to need.'

21. Retirement of the receiver

A receiver may wish to retire through ill health or old age. In this situation, application can be to the court using form CP9.

22. Death of the receiver

The personal representatives of a deceased receiver should notify the court immediately. A final account may have to be prepared.

23. Recovery of the patient

It may be that the patient will recover, in which event application can be made for an order determining the proceedings. Medical evidence that the patient has recovered will be required.

Rule 37(1) CPR 1994 provides that where at any stage of proceedings relating to a patient the court has reason to believe that the patient has recovered, it may require medical evidence of the recovery to be furnished by such person as it thinks appropriate.

In *Re WLW* [1972] 2 All ER 433 there was a conflict of evidence as to whether the patient had recovered. The report of a medical visitor had been disclosed, and it was held that the visitor could be cross-examined about the report. Goff J said at page 438:

'Accordingly, in my judgment, although the judge has a discretion it can only be exercised so as to refuse cross-examination where, on the facts of the particular case, it would be injurious to the patient and such cases could only be rare and exceptional.'

24. Death of the patient

The powers of the receiver terminate with the death of the patient. However, the receiver will have to produce a final account, unless the personal representatives or the persons entitled to the residuary estate agree in writing that it should not be produced.

Rule 37(2) CPR 1994 provides that where at any stage of proceedings relating to a patient, the Public Trustee has reason to believe that the patient has died, he may require evidence of the death to be furnished by such person as he thinks appropriate.

The court will release funds to the personal representatives once final directions have been given. Funds for the payment of funeral accounts, Inheritance Tax and the fees payable to the Probate Registry can be released.

(See Factsheet 4 published by the Court of Protection.)

25. Time limits

Rule 4(1) CPR 1994 provides that where a period of time fixed by the rules or by any order or direction of the court for doing an act expires on a day on which the appropriate office for doing that act is closed and for that reason the act cannot be done on that day, the act shall be in time if done on the next day on which that office is open.

Rule 4(2) provides that where the act is required to be done within a specified period after or from a specified date, the period begins immediately after that date. Rule 4(3) provides that where any period of time fixed as mentioned in r 4(1) is less than six days, any day on which the appropriate office is closed shall not be included in the computation of that period.

Rule 5 empowers the court to extend or abridge time.

26. Power of the court to intervene

The court has power to intervene if it is dissatisfied with the conduct of any proceedings or the carrying out of any order (r 51(1)). Rule 51(2) empower the court to direct any person to make any application and to conduct any proceedings and carry out any directions which the court may specify. If the Official Solicitor consents, he can be appointed to act as solicitor for the patient in the proceedings in place of any solicitor previously acting for him.

27. Fees

Rules 78–86 and the Appendix to the CPR 1994 prescribe the fees payable. In general terms, a fee is payable on the commencement of any proceedings, annually and for transactions.

28. Costs

It will be remembered that r 45 CPR 1994 provides for the remuneration of the receiver (see page 152). Rule 84(7) provides that any other costs are in the discretion of the court – the court may order them to be paid by the patient or charged on or paid out of his estate or paid by any other person attending or taking part in the proceedings.

Rule 90(1) provides that no receiver for a patient, other than the

Public Trustee or the Official Solicitor, is entitled at the expense of the patient's estate to employ a solicitor or other professional person to do any work not usually requiring professional assistance. The court can authorise payment in this situation. Rule 90(2) provides that where two or more persons having the same interest in relation to the matter to be determined attend any hearing by separate legal representatives, they will not be allowed more than one set of costs of the hearing unless the court certifies that the circumstances justify separate representation.

29. Is it possible to avoid an application for the appointment of a receiver?

The procedure for dealing with small estates has already been mentioned (see page 147). If the patient has no assets, it will frequently be unnecessary to apply to the court for the appointment of a receiver. For example, it may be that a pension can be paid to the relatives of a mentally disordered person. In addition, if an enduring power has been granted, application will not be necessary.

30. Money due for past maintenance

Rule 38 CPR 1994 provides that the amount due to any public authority for the past maintenance of a patient may, unless the Public Trustee otherwise directs, be proved by the filing of an account certified under the hand of the proper officer of the authority.

31. Copies of documents

Any person who has filed an affidavit is entitled to a copy of it (r 77(1)). The person having the conduct of the proceedings is entitled on request to be supplied with a copy of any order, certificate, authority, direction, or other document made, given or prepared by the court or the Public Trustee in the proceedings (r 77(2)). The court or the Public Trustee may direct otherwise under both sub-rules.

Rule 77(3) provides that any other person may, on request, be supplied with a copy of any such document as is mentioned in r 77(1) or (2), if the court is satisfied that he has good reason for requiring it and that it is not reasonably practicable for him to obtain it from the person entitled to bespeak a copy from the court or the Public Trustee.

Are relatives entitled to see documents in the possession of the Official Solicitor? In *Re E (mental health patient)* [1985] 1 All ER 609 the Official Solicitor had successfully brought a claim against an area health authority on behalf of a patient. The parents of the patient were not satisfied with the award, and requested the Official Solicitor to release the papers relating to the case. The Court of Appeal confirmed that the paramount consideration was the interest and benefit of the patient (page 615). Stephenson LJ said at pages 616–617:

> '... where, as here, the papers of which the patient seeks inspection are in the custody of the Official Solicitor in connection with litigation in which he has been authorised by the Court of Protection, ..., or in which he is, as he is entitled to be under the Rules of the Supreme Court, the next friend of a patient whose property is being administered by the Court of Protection, a parent of this patient has no absolute right to see those papers, although they are the patient's property, but must obtain the authority of the Court of Protection to order disclosure of them as necessary or expedient for the benefit of the patient. The right course is ... for the Vice-Chancellor ... to inspect the papers himself, thereafter allowing inspection by the father's solicitors of any papers not really harmful to the patient'.

32. Consent to medical treatment

The Court of Protection has no power to agree to medical treatment on behalf of a patient. However, the High Court has jurisdiction under RSC O 15 r 16, or has inherent jurisdiction, to make a declaration as to the legality of a particular operation (*F* v *West Berkshire Health Authority and another (Mental Health Act Commission intervening)* [1989] 2 All ER 545).

33. Relationship between the Court of Protection and the Chancery Division

Does the Chancery Division have power to deal with the estates of persons suffering from mental disorder? The answer is to a large extent in the negative. The matter was raised in *Re K's Settlement Trusts* [1969] 2 Ch 1 where X was entitled under various trusts to a large sum of money on attaining majority. X, whose mental age was unlikely to exceed fifteen, lived abroad. Trustees applied to the Chancery Division for an order that the capital should be retained until a specified date. They also requested an order that the income should be paid to the testamentary guardians for X so that it could be applied for his maintenance and benefit. It was held that the Chancery Division only had jurisdiction if three conditions were satisfied:

- Proceedings in the Court of Protection are not contemplated.
- The income is so small that it will all be used in the maintenance of the beneficiary.
- The Chancery Division must already be seised of the case.

Even if the conditions are satisfied, the jurisdiction is discretionary.

34. Can a creditor enforce a judgment against the patient?

Section 95(2) Mental Health Act 1983 provides that the requirements of the patient must first be considered. The rules of law restricting the enforcement by a creditor of rights against property under the control of the judge in lunacy apply to the property under the control of the judge. However, the interests of creditors must be considered, together with the desirability of making provision for obligations of the patient notwithstanding that they may not be legally enforceable.

Rule 6(2) CPR 1994 provides that if the Public Trustee considers that it may be appropriate to restrict the right of creditors under s 95(2) of the Act, or that payment should be made to persons other than the patient where the patient is insolvent, he must refer the matter to the court for determination.

The patient may owe money to various creditors. A creditor cannot levy execution against the goods of the patient, but the court will make an order for the payment of maintenance for the patient, although not for the spouse of the patient, and this will be without prejudice to any charge or priority the creditor may have acquired by lodging his writ of fi fa with the sheriff (*In re Winkle* [1894] 2 Ch 519).

35. Effect of bankruptcy of the patient

A patient can be made bankrupt, but the trustee in bankruptcy stands in the shoes of the debtor, and cannot obtain a better title. The Court of Protection controls the property of the patient, although if the patient recovers, control will then vest in the trustee in bankruptcy (*Re A Debtor* [1941] 3 All ER 11).

36. Divorce

It may be desirable for a patient to begin proceedings for divorce. This issue was discussed in *Re W* [1970] 2 All ER 502, where sections of the Mental Health Act 1959 similar to those in the

Mental Health Act 1983 were considered.

Section 95(1) Mental Health Act 1983, which re-enacts s 102(1) Mental Health Act 1959, provides:

'The judge may, with respect to the property and affairs of a patient, do or secure the doing of all such things as appear necessary or expedient –

(a) for the maintenance or other benefit of the patient;

(b) for the maintenance or other benefit of members of the patient's family;

(c) for making provision for other persons or purposes for whom or which the patient might be expected to provide if he were not mentally disordered; or

(d) otherwise for administering the patient's affairs.

It was held that 'benefit ... is not restricted to material benefit, but that it is of wide significance comprehending whatever would be beneficial in any respect, material or otherwise' (Ungoed-Thomas J at page 505). At page 507 he said:

'Various aspects of "benefit", or factors in assessing "benefit", were discussed before me: (1) breakdown of marriage; (2) religion; (3) public policy; (4) children; (5) financial consequences; (6) the effect of the Divorce Reform Act 1969. These are of course all clearly factors to be taken into consideration in deciding whether or not, on balance, the presentation of a petition is for the "benefit" of the objects sought by the Act to be benefited, having regard to the order of priority laid down by the Act. The weight to be attached to the different factors will vary with the circumstances as variously as the circumstances themselves will vary ...'.

The spouse of a patient may wish to apply for financial provision from the estate of a patient. This can be done (*Re CL v CFW* [1928] P 223).

37. Preservation of interests in the patient's property

It may be that a person would have been entitled to some property of the patient, which is disposed of under the Act. In these circumstances, the disappointed beneficiary takes the same interest, if and so far as circumstances allow, in any property belonging to the estate of the deceased which represents the property disposed of (s 101 Mental Health Act 1983).

38. Reviews and appeals

Rule 56(1) CPR 1994 provides that any person who is aggrieved by a decision of the court not made on a hearing, or a decision of the Public Trustee, may apply to the court within eight days of the date on which the decision was given to have the decision reviewed by the court. On the hearing of the application the court may either confirm or revoke the previous decision or make any other order or decision which it thinks fit (r 56(3)). Note that no appeal lies from a decision under r 86, which deals with the remission, postponement and exemption of fees (r 56(2)).

Rule 57 provides for appeals from decisions made after a hearing. The appellant must within fourteen days:

(a) serve a notice of appeal in Form D on –

(i) every person who appeared, or was represented, before the court when the order or decision was made or given, and

(ii) any other person whom the court may direct; and

(b) lodge a copy of the notice at the court office.

The time and place at which the appeal is to be heard is fixed by the court. Notice of the time and place so fixed is sent to the appellant who must immediately send notice of it to every person who has been served with notice of the appeal (r 57(3)). Rule 57(4) provides that no evidence further to that given at the hearing shall be filed in support of or in opposition to the appeal without leave of the court.

39. Representation by solicitors

Problems can sometimes arise if more than one solicitor is instructed. For example, two relatives of a mentally disordered person may instruct different solicitors. According to a Practice Direction issued by the Court of Protection on 9 August 1995 the solicitor who makes the first application will be regarded as acting for the patient or the donor of an enduring power, until there is an objection to the application, or another application is received. The first solicitor must then choose whether to represent the first applicant or the patient. If the solicitor chooses to represent the first applicant, it will be necessary for the court to decide if the patient should be represented by another solicitor. The Official Solicitor may be appointed if he agrees.

***

Summary

- The Court of Protection has wide powers to deal with the property of a mentally disordered person.
- Application for the appointment of a receiver must be supported by a medical certificate and a certificate of family and property.
- There is a short procedure for small estates.
- A person appointed as receiver must give security.
- A receiver must keep accounts.
- Visitors may be asked to make further inquiries.

Chapter 15

Wills for mentally disordered persons

1. Testamentary capacity of the donor of a power of attorney

The mere fact that a donor has granted an ordinary or enduring power will not prevent him making a valid will, provided he has the necessary testamentary capacity. In *Banks v Goodfellow* (1870) LR 5 QB 549 at page 565 Cockburn CJ stated:

> 'It is essential ... that a testator shall understand the nature of the act and its effects; shall understand the extent of the property of which he is disposing; shall be able to comprehend and appreciate the claims to which he ought to give effect; and, with a view to the latter object, that no disorder of the mind shall poison his affections, pervert his sense of right, or prevent the exercise of his natural faculties – that no insane delusion shall influence his will in disposing of his property and bring about a disposal of it which, if the mind had been sound, would not have been made.'

If an enduring power is granted, the donee must apply for registration of the power if he has reason to believe that the donor is or is becoming mentally incapable (s 4(1) EPAA 1985). Even if the power is registered, if the donor recovers his mental capacity, he can make a valid will, even though the registration has not been cancelled. It is possible that the donor might still have the capacity to make a will even though the donee is under a duty to apply for registration because the donor is becoming mentally incapable. A donor may have good days when he has capacity to make a will, and bad days when he lacks capacity.

2. Wills under the Mental Health Act 1983

(a) Jurisdiction

An attorney under an ordinary power or an enduring power of attorney cannot make a will on behalf of the donor of the power.

If the donor lacks capacity to make a will, application can be made to the Court of Protection, which is empowered by s 96(1) Mental Health Act 1983 to:

'make orders and give directions or authorities for ... (e) the execution for the patient of a will making any provision (whether by way of disposing of property or exercising a power or otherwise) which could be made by a will executed by the patient if he were not mentally disordered.'

Under s 94(2) Mental Health Act 1983, the judge can exercise his functions 'where after considering medical evidence, he is satisfied that a person is incapable, by reason of mental disorder, of managing and administering his property and affairs'.

Section 96(4) provides that the power of a judge to make or give an order, direction or authority for the execution of a will for a patient must not be exercised unless the judge has reason to believe that the patient is incapable of making a valid will for himself.

There is no need to apply for the appointment of a receiver at the same time as an application for a statutory will (see PD Lewis, *The Law Society's Gazette* (29 April 1987) at page 1219).

(b) Beneficiaries

This is dealt with in s 95(1) Mental Health Act 1983. The will can benefit members of the patient's family, and also persons for whom the patient might be expected to provide if he were not mentally disordered. 'Family' is not defined in the 1983 Act, but it does not include collateral relatives such as nephews and nieces (*Re DML* [1965] 2 All ER 129). Relatives such as a spouse, issue or parents are clearly members of the family, but other relatives will have to prove that they are persons for whom the patient might have been expected to provide had he not been mentally disordered.

(c) Principles

In *Re D (J)* [1982] Ch 237 at pages 243, 244, it was held that the judge will apply the following five principles in deciding what will should be made for the patient:

(i) 'it is to be assumed that the patient is having a brief lucid interval at the time when the will was made';

(ii) 'during the lucid interval the patient has a full knowledge of the past and a full realisation that as soon as the will is executed he or she will relapse into the actual mental state that

169

previously existed, with the prognosis as it actually is';

(iii) 'it is the actual patient who has to be considered and not a hypothetical patient';

(iv) 'during the hypothetical lucid interval, the patient is to be envisaged as being advised by competent solicitors';

 (v) 'in all normal cases the patient is to be envisaged as taking a broad brush to the claims on his bounty, rather than an accountant's pen'.

In *Re C* [1991] The Independent 2 May, the patient had always been mentally incapable. Hoffmann J said that 'the court must assume that she would have been a normal decent person, acting in accordance with contemporary standards of morality'.

If appropriate, application can be made for a will in order to save tax (*Re L (WLG)* [1966] 1 Ch 135).

(d) Applications to the court

The procedure is governed by the Court of Protection Rules 1994 (SI 1994 No 3046) and Practice Notes issued by the Court of Protection.

Rule 20 provides that applications can be made by:

 (i) the receiver for the patient; or

 (ii) any person who has made an application for the appointment of a receiver which has not been determined; or

(iii) any person who under any known will of the patient or under his intestacy may become entitled to any property of the patient or any interest therein; or

(iv) any person for whom the patient might be expected to provide if he were not mentally disordered; or

 (v) an attorney acting under a registered enduring power; or

(vi) any other person whom the court may authorise to make it or, where it relates to a function to be exercised by him, the Public Trustee may authorise to make it.

Rule 21 deals with who should be given notice of the hearing, and the time limits for doing so. It provides:

'(1) Except where these rules provide otherwise or the court directs otherwise the applicant shall give notice of the hearing of an application in accordance with the following provisions of this rule.

(2) Where a receiver has been appointed for a patient he shall,

unless he is the applicant, be given notice of the hearing of any application relating to the patient ...

(4) Notice of the hearing of the application shall also be given to such other persons who appear to the court to be interested as the court may specify.'

Rule 21(5) provides that notice of the hearing of an application for the execution of a will of the patient must be given not less than two clear days before the date fixed for the hearing.

If the court thinks that the interests of the patient are not adequately represented by the receiver, the court can direct the Official Solicitor to act as solicitor for the patient, provided that the Official Solicitor consents (r 15).

It may be that no notice is appropriate. In *Re Davey* [1980] 3 All ER 342 an elderly lady made a will benefiting seventeen named persons. Subsequently, a psychiatrist examined her, and concluded that she was incapable of managing her own affairs. She then married a forty-eight-year-old man who worked at the nursing home where she lived; the effect of the marriage was to revoke the will, and the man would have been entitled to a substantial part of the estate under the intestacy rules. The matter came to the attention of the Court of Protection on 17 December 1979, and on 20 December 1979 the Court directed the execution of a will in the same form as the original one. It was held that it was not necessary for notice to have been given to the man. Fox J said at page 348:

'No doubt in the normal case the court would generally insist on the joinder of a person who was adversely affected by the relief sought, but in circumstances of urgency the position may be different. The deputy master quite clearly directed his mind to the question of whether Mr Davey should be joined as a respondent and decided against it on the ground of delay. In the circumstances I think that that was a reasonable view for the deputy master to take.'

Service should be effected personally, although the court can direct that any notice should be served by sending it by first class post to the last known address of the person to be served (r 22). A solicitor can accept service (r 23). Under r 25(1)(b) if the patient is required to be served, service must be made on his receiver, or if there is no receiver, on the person acting in pursuance of an order or direction made under rule 9, or, if there is no such person, on an attorney acting under a registered power of attorney, or, if there is no such attorney, on the person with whom he resides or in whose care he is.

(e) Evidence

An affidavit must be filed. Practice Note 9 provides details of the information which should be included.

(f) Execution of the will

The judge may authorise a person to execute a will on behalf of a patient. Under s 97(1)(a) Mental Health Act 1983, the will must be signed by the authorised person with the name of the patient, and with his own name, in the presence of two or more witnesses present at the same time. In addition, the will must be attested and subscribed by those witnesses in the presence of the authorised person, and sealed with the Official Seal of the Court of Protection.

Summary

- The donor of an enduring power can execute a will provided he has the necessary capacity.
- The donee of a power of attorney cannot make a will for the donor.
- If the donor of a power lacks capacity to execute a will, application can be made to the Court of Protection for the execution of a will.
- The beneficiaries under such a will can be members of the patient's family, and also persons for whom the patient might be expected to provide.

Appendix 1

Precedents

Contents

1. General power of attorney under the Powers of Attorney Act 1971

This general power of attorney is made this ..... day of ..... 19 .....
by (*name of donor of power*) ....
of ....
I appoint ....
of ....
[or .... of .... and .... of
jointly or jointly and severally] to be my attorney[s] in accordance with
section 10 of the Powers of Attorney Act 1971.

In Witness whereof (the donor) has hereunto set his hand and seal the day
and year above written.

Signed as a deed and delivered: ....

Witness: ....

© *Crown Copyright*

2. Limited power of attorney authorising sale of a house and the purchase and mortgage of another house

This limited power of attorney is made this ..... day of ..... 19 .....
by ....
of ....

I appoint ....
of ....
to do all or any of the following acts:

1. To sign a contract and execute a conveyance or transfer for the sale
    of ....
    at a price of not less £ ....

2. To pay to .... such money as is necessary to redeem the
    charge or charges or mortgage or mortgages in their favour

3. To sign a contract and execute a conveyance or transfer for the
    purchase of .... at a price not exceeding £ ....

4. To execute a charge or mortgage of .... in favour of
    the .... for an amount not exceeding £ ....

5. To draw whatever cheques shall be necessary.

6. To do such other acts as shall be necessary to complete the sale,

redemption of the existing charges or mortgages, the purchase and mortgage or charge.

Signed as a deed and delivered: ....

Witness: ....

3. Limited power of attorney authorising the redemption of an existing mortgage and the remortgage of the property

Opening – as in precedent 2.

1. To pay to .... such money as is necessary to redeem the charge or charges or mortgage or mortgages in their favour on ....

2. To draw whatever cheques shall be necessary for this purpose in favour of ....

3. To execute a charge or mortgage on the security of in favour of ....

4. To do such other acts as shall be necessary to complete the redemption of the existing charges or mortgages and to complete the charge or mortgage in favour.

Signed as a deed and delivered: ....

Witness: ....

4. Limited power of attorney authorising the grant of a lease

Opening – as in precedent 2.

1. To grant a lease of [insert address of property] for a term not exceeding .... years on such terms as my attorney thinks fit.

2. To receive the rent and to apply the rent in discharge of the obligations of the landlord.

3. To take such proceedings as may be necessary to recover any rent or to enforce any of the obligations imposed on the tenant or to recover possession of the property.

Signed as a deed and delivered: ....

Witness: ....

5. Statutory declaration under the Land Registration (Powers of Attorney) Rules 1986 – powers other than enduring powers

I, ...

of ....
do solemnly and sincerely declare:

1. On .... day of .... 19 ...., I completed the purchase of .... [the property].

2. The vendor had granted a power of attorney to (*insert name of donee*) by a deed dated the .... day of .... 199 ....

3. The property is registered at H.M. Land Registry under title number .... (*Delete if title is unregistered.*)

4. At the time of the completion of the purchase I did not know of any revocation of the power or of any event (such as the death, bankruptcy or other incapacity of the donor) which had the effect of revoking the power.

And I make this solemn declaration conscientiously believing the same to be true and by the virtue of the Statutory Declarations Act 1835

Declared at ....

this .... day of .... 199 ....

Before me, ...

6. Statutory declaration under the Land Registration (Powers of Attorney) Rules 1986 – enduring powers of attorney

I, ...

of ....
do solemnly and sincerely declare:

1. On the ..... day of ..... 19....., I completed the purchase of ......
   ....
   [the property].

2. The vendor had granted a power of attorney to [insert name of donee] by a deed dated the .... day of .... 199.........

3. The property is registered at H.M. Land Registry under title number .... (Delete if title is unregistered.)

4. At the time of completion of the purchase I did not know:

> (a) of any revocation of the power whether by the donor or by an Order of the Court of Protection
>
> (b) of the occurrence of any event (such as death of the donor or the bankruptcy of the donor or of any donee or a direction by the Court of Protection on exercising its powers under Part VII of the Mental Health Act 1983) which had the effect of revoking the power
>
> (c) that the power was not a valid enduring power of attorney and had been revoked by the donor's mental incapacity.

Conclusion – as in precedent 5.

7. Delegation of trusts by power of attorney under section 25 Trustee Act 1925

This power of attorney is made this .... day of .... 199 ....
by ....
of ....
I appoint ....
of ....
to execute or exercise all or any of the trusts powers and discretions vested in me either alone or jointly with any other person or persons for the period of twelve months from the date hereof.

Signed as a deed and delivered: ....

Witness: ....

8. Notice under section 25(4) Trustee Act 1925

To ....
of ....

By a power of attorney coming into force on the ..... day of ......
199 ...., I delegated the execution or exercise of the trusts powers and discretions vested in me for a period of .... months to ....

of ....

The power has been given because I (*state reason*).

9. Extension of powers in respect of shareholdings

Clauses to be incorporated in ordinary or enduring powers:

To permit a stockbroker or other suitably qualified person to buy and sell shares in his absolute discretion without being liable for any losses.

To permit shares to be held in the name of a nominee without being liable for any losses.

Appendix 2

1. Powers of Attorney Act 1971

Arrangement of sections

Schedules

Execution of powers of attorney

1.-(1) An instrument creating a power of attorney shall be executed as a deed by the donor of the power.

(2) Repealed by Law of Property (Miscellaneous Provisions) Act 1989.

(3) This section is without prejudice to any requirement in, or having effect under, any other Act as to the witnessing of instruments creating powers of attorney and does not affect the rules relating to the execution of instruments by bodies corporate.

Abolition of deposit or filing of instruments creating powers of attorney

2.-(1) As from the commencement of this Act no instrument creating a power of attorney, and no copy of any such instrument, shall be deposited or filed at the central office of the Supreme Court or at the Land Registry under section 25 of the Trustee Act 1925, section 125 of the Law of Property Act 1925 or section 219 of the Supreme Court or Judicature (Consolidation) Act 1925.

(2) This section does not affect any right to search for, inspect or copy, or to obtain an office copy of, any such document which has been deposited or filed as aforesaid before the commencement of this Act.

Proof of instruments creating powers of attorney

3.-(1) The contents of an instrument creating a power of attorney may be proved by means of a copy which –

(a)   is a reproduction of the original made with a photographic or other device for reproducing documents in facsimile; and

(b)   contains the following certificate or certificates signed by the donor of the power or by a solicitor or stockbroker, that is to say

     (i) a certificate at the end to the effect that the copy is a true and complete copy of the original; and

     (ii) if the original consists of two or more pages, a certificate at the end of each page of the copy to the effect that it is a true and complete copy of the corresponding page of the original.

(2) Where a copy of an instrument creating a power of attorney has been made which complies with subsection (1) of this section, the contents of the instruments may also be proved by means of a copy of that copy if the further copy itself complies with that subsection, taking references in it to the original as references to the copy from which the further copy is made.

(3) In this section 'stockbroker' means a member of any stock exchange within the meaning of the Stock Transfer Act 1963 or the Stock Transfer Act (Northern Ireland) 1963.

(4) This section is without prejudice to section 4 of the Evidence and Powers of Attorney Act 1940 (proof of deposited instruments by office copy) and to any other method of proof authorised by law.

(5) For the avoidance of doubt, in relation to an instrument made in Scotland the references to a power of attorney in this section and in section 4 of the Evidence and Powers of Attorney Act 1940 include references to a factory and commission.

Powers of attorney given as security

4.-(1) Where a power of attorney is expressed to be irrevocable and is given to secure –

(a)   a proprietary interest of the donee of the power; or

(b)   the performance of an obligation owed to the donee,

then, so long as the donee has that interest or the obligation remains undischarged, the power shall not be revoked –

> (i) by the donor without the consent of the donee; or
>
> (ii) by the death, incapacity or bankruptcy of the donor or, if the donor is a body corporate, by its winding up or dissolution.

(2) A power of attorney given to secure a proprietary interest may be given to the person entitled to the interest and persons deriving title under him to that interest, and those persons shall be duly constituted donees of the power for all purposes of the power but without prejudice to any right to appoint substitutes given by the power.

(3) This section applies to powers of attorney whenever created.

Protection of donee and third persons where the power of attorney is revoked

5.-(1) A donee of a power of attorney who acts in pursuance of the power at a time when it has been revoked shall not, by reason of the revocation, incur any liability (either to the donor or to any other person) if at that time he did not know that the power had been revoked.

(2) Where a power of attorney has been revoked and a person, without knowledge of the revocation, deals with the donee of the power, the transaction between them shall, in favour of that person, be as valid as if the power had then been in existence.

(3) Where the power is expressed in the instrument creating it to be irrevocable and to be given by way of security then, unless the person dealing with the donee knows that it was not in fact given by way of security, he shall be entitled to assume that the power is incapable of revocation except by the donor acting with the consent of the donee and shall accordingly be treated for the purposes of subsection (2) of this section as having knowledge of the revocation only if he knows that it has been revoked in that manner.

(4) Where the interest of a purchaser depends on whether a transaction between the donee of a power of attorney and another person was valid by virtue of subsection (2) of this section, it shall be conclusively presumed in favour of the purchaser that that person did not at the material time know of the revocation of the power if –

(a) the transaction between that person and the donee was completed within twelve months of the date on which the power came into operation; or

(b) that person makes a statutory declaration, before or within three months after the completion of the purchase, that he did not at the material time know of the revocation of the power.

(5) Without prejudice to subsection (3) of this section, for the purposes of this section knowledge of the revocation of a power of attorney includes knowledge of the occurrence of any event (such as the death of the donor) which has the effect of revoking the power.

(6) In this section 'purchaser' and 'purchase' have the meanings specified in section 205 (1) of the Law of Property Act 1925.

(7) This section applies whenever the power of attorney was created but only to acts and transactions after the commencement of this Act.

Additional protection for transferees under stock exchange transactions

6.–(1) Without prejudice to section 5 of this Act, where –

(a) the donee of a power of attorney executes, as transferor, an instrument transferring registered securities; and

(b) the instrument is executed for the purposes of a stock exchange transaction,

it shall be conclusively presumed in favour of the transferee that the power had not been revoked at the date of the instrument if a statutory declaration to that effect is made by the donee of the power on or within three months after that date.

(2) In this section 'registered securities' and 'stock exchange transaction' have the same meanings as in the Stock Transfer Act 1963.

Execution of instruments etc. by donee of power of attorney

7.–(1) The donee of a power of attorney may, if he thinks fit –

(a) execute any instrument with his own signature, and

(b) do any other thing in his own name, by the authority of the donor of the power, and any document executed or thing done in that manner shall be as effective as if executed or done by the donee with the signature and seal, or, as the case may be, in the name, of the donor of the power.

(2) For the avoidance of doubt it is hereby declared that an instrument to which subsection (3) of section 74 of the Law of Property Act 1925 applies may be executed either as provided in that subsection or as provided in this section.

(3) This section is without prejudice to any statutory direction requiring an instrument to be executed in the name of an estate owner within the meaning of the said Act of 1925.

(4) This section applies whenever the power of attorney was created.

Repeal of s. 129 of Law of Property Act 1925

8.–Section 129 of the Law of Property Act 1925 (which contains provisions, now unnecessary, in respect of powers of attorney granted by married women) shall cease to have effect.

Power to delegate trusts etc. by power of attorney

9.–(1) Section 25 of the Trustee Act 1925 (power to delegate trusts etc., during absence abroad) shall be amended as follows.

(2) For subsections (1) to (8) of that section there shall be substituted the following subsections –

'(1) Notwithstanding any rule of law or equity to the contrary, a trustee may, by power of attorney, delegate for a period not exceeding twelve months the execution or exercise of all or any of the trusts, powers and discretions vested in him as trustee either alone or jointly with any other person or persons.

(2) The persons who may be donees of a power of attorney under this section include a trust corporation but not (unless a trust corporation) the only other co-trustee of the donor of the power.

(3) An instrument creating a power of attorney under this section shall be attested by at least one witness.

(4) Before or within seven days after giving a power of attorney under this section the donor shall give written notice thereof (specifying the date on which the power comes into operation and its duration, the donee of the power, the reason why the power is given and, where some only are delegate, the trusts, powers and discretions delegated) to –

(a) each person (other than himself) if any, who under any instrument creating the trust has power (whether alone or jointly) to appoint a new trustee; and

(b) each of the other trustees, if any;

but failure to comply with this subsection shall not, in favour of a person dealing with the donee of the power, invalidate any act done or instrument executed by the donee.

(5) The donor of a power of attorney given under this section shall be liable for the acts or defaults of the donee in the same manner as if they were the acts or defaults of the donor.'

(3) Subsections (9) and (10) of the said section 25 shall stand as subsections (6) and (7) and for subsection (11) of that section there shall be substituted the following subsection –

'(8) This section applies to a personal representative, tenant for life and statutory owner as it applies to a trustee except that subsection (4) shall apply as if it is required the notice there mentioned to be given –

(a)   in the case of a personal representative, to each of the other personal representatives, if any, except any executor who has renounced probate;

(b)   in the case of a tenant for life, to the trustees of the settlement and to each person, if any, who together with the person giving the notice constitutes the tenant for life;

(c)   in the case of a statutory owner, to each of the persons, if any, who together with the person giving the notice constitute the statutory owner and, in the case of a statutory owner by virtue of section 23(1)(a) of the Settled Land Act 1925, to the trustees of the settlement.'

(4) This section applies whenever the trusts, powers or discretions in question arose but does not invalidate anything done by virtue of the said section 25 as in force at the commencement of this Act.

Effect of general power of attorney in specified form

10.–(1) Subject to subsection (2) of this section, a general power of attorney in the form set out in Schedule 1 to this Act, or in a form to the like effect but expressed to be made under this Act, shall operate to confer –

(a)   on the donee of the power; or

(b)   if there is more than one donee, on the donees acting jointly or severally, as the case may be,

authority to do on behalf of the donor anything which he can lawfully do by an attorney.

(2) This section does not apply to functions which the donor has as a trustee or personal representative or as a tenant for life or statutory owner within the meaning of the Settled Land Act 1925.

Short title, repeals, consequential amendments, commencement and extent

11.–(1) This Act may be cited as the Powers of Attorney Act 1971.

(2) The enactments specified in Schedule 2 to this Act are hereby repealed to the extent specified in the third column of that Schedule.

(3) In section 125 (2) of the Law of Property Act 1925 for the words 'as aforesaid' there shall be substituted the words 'under the Land Registration Act 1925'; and in section 219 (2) of the Supreme Court of Judicature (Consolidation) Act 1925 for the words 'so deposited' there shall be substituted the words 'deposited under this section before the commencement of the Powers of Attorney Act 1971.'

(4) This Act shall come into force on 1st October 1971.

(5) Section 3 of this Act extends to Scotland and Northern Ireland but, save as aforesaid, this Act extends to England and Wales only.

Schedules

Section 10   SCHEDULE 1

FORM OF GENERAL POWER OF ATTORNEY FOR PURPOSES OF SECTION 10

THIS   GENERAL   POWER   OF   ATTORNEY   is   made   this
.... day of .... 19..... by AB of ....
I appoint CD of .... [*or* CD of .... and EF of .... jointly *or*
jointly and severally] to be my attorney[s] in accordance with section
10 of the Powers of Attorney Act 1971.
IN WITNESS etc,

[*Schedule 2 concerns repeals and is not reproduced.*]
© *Crown copyright. Reproduced with the permission of the Controller of HMSO.*

2. Enduring Powers of Attorney Act 1985

Arrangement of sections

Enduring powers of attorney

Enduring power of attorney to survive mental incapacity of donor

1.–(1) Where an individual creates a power of attorney which is an enduring power within the meaning of this Act then –

(a)   the power shall not be revoked by any subsequent mental incapacity of his; but

(b)   upon such incapacity supervening the donee of the power may not do anything under the authority of the power except as provided by subsection (2) below or as directed or authorised by the court under section 5 unless or, as the case may be, until the instrument creating the power is registered by the court under section 6; and

(c)   section 5 of the Powers of Attorney Act 1971 (protection of donee and third persons) so far as applicable shall apply if and so long as paragraph (b) above operates to suspend the donee's authority to act under the power as if the power had been revoked by the donor's mental incapacity.

(2) Notwithstanding subsection (1)(b) above, where the attorney has made an application for registration of the instrument then, until the application has been initially determined, the attorney may take action under the power –

(a)   to maintain the donor or prevent loss to his estate; or

(b)   to maintain himself or other persons in so far as section 3(4) permits him to do so.

(3) Where the attorney purports to act as provided by subsection (2) above then, in favour of a person who deals with him without knowledge that the attorney is acting otherwise than in accordance with paragraph (a) or (b) of that subsection, the transaction between them shall be as valid as if the attorney were acting in accordance with paragraph (a) or (b).

Characteristics of an enduring power

2.–(1) Subject to subsections (7) to (9) below and section 11, a power of attorney is an enduring power within the meaning of this Act if the instrument which creates the power –

(a)   is in the prescribed form; and

(b)   was executed in the prescribed manner by the donor and the attorney; and

(c)   incorporated at the time of execution by the donor the prescribed explanatory information.

(2) The Lord Chancellor shall make regulations as to the form and execution of instruments creating enduring powers and the regulations shall contain such provisions as appear to him to be appropriate for securing –

(a)   that no document is used to create an enduring power which does not incorporate such information explaining the general effect of creating or accepting the power as may be prescribed; and

(b)   that such instruments include statements to the following effect –

   (i)   by the donor, that he intends the power to continue in spite of any supervening mental incapacity of his;

   (ii)   by the donor, that he read or had read to him the information explaining the effect of creating the power;

   (iii)   by the attorney, that he understands the duty of registration imposed by this Act.

(3) Regulations under subsection (2) above –

(a)   may include different provision for cases where more than one attorney is to be appointed by the instrument than for cases where only one attorney is to be appointed; and

(b)   may, if they amend or revoke any regulations previously made under that subsection, include saving and transitional provisions.

(4) Regulations under subsection (2) above shall be made by statutory instrument which shall be subject to annulment in pursuance of a resolution of either House of Parliament.

(5) An instrument in the prescribed form purporting to have been executed in the prescribed manner shall be taken, in the absence of evidence to the contrary, to be a document which incorporated at the time of execution by the donor the prescribed explanatory information.

(6) Where an instrument differs in an immaterial respect in form of mode of expression from the prescribed form the instrument shall be treated as sufficient in point of form and expression.

(7) A power of attorney cannot be an enduring power unless, when he executes the instrument creating it, the attorney is –

(a)   an individual who has attained eighteen years and is not bankrupt; or

(b)   a trust corporation.

(8) A power of attorney under section 25 of the Trustee Act 1925 (power to delegate trusts etc. by power of attorney) cannot be an enduring power.

(9) A power of attorney which gives the attorney a right to appoint a substitute or successor cannot be an enduring power.

(10) An enduring power shall be revoked by the bankruptcy of the attorney whatever the circumstances of the bankruptcy.

(11) An enduring power shall be revoked on the exercise by the court of any of its powers under Part VII of the Mental Health Act 1983 if, but only if, the court so directs.

(12) No disclaimer of an enduring power, whether by deed or otherwise, shall be valid unless and until the attorney gives notice of it to the donor or, where section 4(6) or 7(1) applies, to the court.

(13) In this section 'prescribed' means prescribed under subsection (2) above.

Scope of authority etc. of attorney under enduring power

3.-(1) An enduring power may confer general authority (as defined in subsection (2) below) on the attorney to act on the donor's behalf in relation to all or a specified part of the property and affairs of the donor or may confer on him authority to do specified things on the donor's behalf and the authority may, in either case, be conferred subject to conditions and restrictions.

(2) Where an instrument is expressed to confer general authority on the attorney it operates to confer, subject to the restriction imposed by subsection (5) below and to any conditions or restrictions contained in the instrument, authority to do on behalf of the donor anything which the donor can lawfully do by an attorney.

(3) Subject to any conditions or restrictions contained in the instrument, an attorney under an enduring power, whether general or limited, may (without obtaining any consent) execute or exercise all or any of the trusts, powers or discretions vested in the donor as trustee and may (without the concurrence of any other person) give a valid receipt for capital or other money paid.

(4) Subject to any other conditions or restrictions contained in the instrument, an attorney under an enduring power, whether general or limited, may (without obtaining any consent) act under the power so as to benefit himself or other persons than the donor to the following extent but no further, that is to say –

(a)   he may so act in relation to himself or in relation to any other person if the donor might be expected to provide for his or that person's needs respectively; and

(b)   he may do whatever the donor might be expected to do to meet those needs.

(5) Without prejudice to subsection (4) above but subject to any conditions or restrictions contained in the instrument, an attorney under an enduring power, whether general or limited, may (without obtaining any consent) dispose of the property of the donor by way of gift to the following extent but no further, that is to say –

(a)   he may make gifts of a seasonal nature or at a time, or on an anniversary, of a birth or marriage, to persons (including himself) who are related to or connected with the donor, and

(b)   he may make gifts to any charity to whom the donor made or might be expected to make gifts,

provided that the value of each such gift is not unreasonable having regard to all the circumstances and in particular the size of the donor's estate.

Action on actual or impending incapacity of donor

Duties of attorney in event of actual or impending incapacity of donor

4.–(1) If the attorney under an enduring power has reason to believe that the donor is or is becoming mentally incapable subsections (2) to (6) below shall apply.

(2) The attorney shall, as soon as practicable, make an application to the court for the registration of the instrument creating the power.

(3) Before making an application for registration the attorney shall comply with the provisions as to notice set out in Schedule 1.

(4) An application for registration shall be made in the prescribed form and shall contain such statements as may be prescribed.

(5) The attorney may, before making an application for the registration of the instrument, refer to the court for its determination any question as to the validity of the power and he shall comply with any direction given to him by the court on that determination.

(6) No disclaimer of the power shall be valid unless and until the attorney gives notice of it to the court.

(7) Any person who, in an application for registration, makes a statement which he knows to be false in a material particular shall be liable –

(a)   on conviction on indictment, to imprisonment for a term not exceeding two years or to a fine, or both; and

(b)   on summary conviction, to imprisonment for a term not exceeding six months or to a fine exceeding the statutory maximum, or both.

(8) In this section and Schedule 1 'prescribed' means prescribed by rules of court.

Functions of court prior to registration

5.– Where the court has reason to believe that the donor of an enduring power may be, or may be becoming, mentally incapable and the court is of the opinion that it is necessary, before the instrument creating the power is registered, to exercise any power with respect to the power of attorney or the attorney appointed to act under it which would become exercisable under section 8(2) on its registration, the court may exercise that power under this section and may do so whether the attorney has or has not made an application to the court for the registration of the instrument.

Functions of court on application for registration

6.–(1) In any case where –

(a)   an application for registration is made in accordance with section 4(3) and (4), and

(b)   neither subsection (2) nor subsection (4) below applies,

the court shall register the instrument to which the application relates.

(2) Where it appears to the court that there is in force under Part VII of the Mental Health Act 1983 an order appointing a receiver for the donor but the power has not also been revoked then, unless it directs otherwise, the court shall not exercise or further exercise its functions under this section but shall refuse the application for registration.

(3) Where it appears from an application for registration that notice of it has not been given under Schedule 1 to some person entitled to receive it (other than a person in respect of whom the attorney has been dispensed or is otherwise exempt from the requirement to give notice) the court shall direct that the application be treated for the purposes of this Act as having been made in accordance with section 4(3), if the court is satisfied that, as regards each such person –

(a)   it was undesirable or impracticable for the attorney to give him notice; or

(b)   no useful purpose is likely to be served by giving him notice.

(4) If, in the case of an application for registration –

(a)   a valid notice of objection to the registration is received by the court before the expiry of the period of five weeks beginning with the date or, as the case may be, the latest date on which the attorneys gave notice to any person under Schedule 1, or

(b)   it appears from the application that there is no one to whom notice has been given under paragraph 1 of that Schedule, or

(c)   the court has reason to believe that appropriate inquiries might bring to light evidence on which the court could be satisfied that one of the grounds of objection set out in subsection (5) below was established,

the court shall neither register the instrument nor refuse the application until it has made or caused to be made such inquiries (if any) as it thinks appropriate in the circumstances of the case.

(5) For the purposes of this Act a notice of objection to the registration of an instrument is valid if the objection is made on one or more of the following grounds, namely –

(a)   that the power purported to have been created by the instrument was not valid as an enduring power of attorney;

(b)   that the power created by the instrument no longer subsists;

(c)   that the application is premature because the donor is not yet becoming mentally incapable;

(d)   that fraud or undue pressure was used to induce the donor to create the power;

(e)   that, having regard to all the circumstances and in particular the attorney's relationship to or connection with the donor, the attorney is unsuitable to be the donor's attorney.

(6) If, in a case where subsection (4) above applies, any of the grounds of objection in subsection (5) above is established to the satisfaction of the

court, the court shall refuse the application but if, in such a case, it is not so satisfied, the court shall register the instrument to which the application relates.

(7) Where the court refuses an application for registration on ground (d) or (e) in subsection (5) above it shall by order revoke the power created by the instrument.

(8) Where the court refuses an application for registration on any ground other than that specified in subsection (5)(c) above the instrument shall be delivered up to be cancelled, unless the court otherwise directs.

Legal position after registration

Effect and proof of registration etc.

7.–(1) The effect of the registration of an instrument under section 6 is that –

(a) no revocation of the power by the donee shall be valid unless and until the court confirms the revocation under section 8(3);

(b) no disclaimer of the power shall be valid unless and until the attorney gives notice of it to the court;

(c) the donor may not extend or restrict the scope of the authority conferred by the instrument and no instruction or consent given by him after registration shall, in the case of a consent, confer any right and, in the case of an instruction, impose or confer any obligation or right on or create any liability of the attorney or other persons having notice of the instruction or consent.

(2) Subsection (1) above applies for so long as the instrument is registered under section 6 whether or not the donor is for the time being mentally incapable.

(3) A document purporting to be an office copy of an instrument registered under this Act shall, in any part of the United Kingdom, be evidence of the contents of the instrument and of the fact that it has been so registered.

(4) Subsection (3) above is without prejudice to section 3 of the Powers of Attorney Act 1971 (proof by certified copies) and to any other method of proof authorised by law.

Functions of court with respect to registered power

8.–(1) Where an instrument has been registered under section 6, the court shall have the following functions with respect to the power and the donor of and the attorney appointed to act under the power.

(2) The court may –

(a) determine any question as to the meaning or effect of the instrument;

(b) give directions with respect to –

(i) the management or disposal by the attorney of the property and affairs of the donor;

      (ii)   the rendering of accounts by the attorney and the production of the records kept by him for the purpose;

      (iii) the remuneration or expenses of the attorney, whether or not in default of or in accordance with any provision made by the instrument, including directions for the repayment of excessive or the payment of additional remuneration;

(c)   require the attorney to furnish information or produce documents or things in his possession as attorney;

(d)   give any consent or authorisation to act which the attorney would have to obtain from a mentally capable donor;

(e)   authorise the attorney to act so as to benefit himself or other persons than the donor otherwise than in accordance with section 3(4) and (5) (but subject to any conditions or restrictions contained in the instrument);

(f)   relieve the attorney wholly or partly from any liability which he has or may have incurred on account of a breach of his duties as attorney.

(3) On application made for the purpose by or on behalf of the donor, the court shall confirm the revocation of the power if satisfied that the donor has done whatever is necessary in law to effect an express revocation of the power and was mentally capable of revoking a power of attorney when he did so (whether or not he is so when the court considers the application).

(4) The court shall cancel the registration of an instrument registered under section 6 in any of the following circumstances, that is to say –

(a)   on confirming the revocation of the power under subsection (3) above or receiving notice of disclaimer under section 7(1)(b);

(b)   on giving a direction revoking the power on exercising any of its powers under Part VII of the Mental Health Act 1983;

(c)   on being satisfied that the donor is and is likely to remain mentally capable;

(d)   on being satisfied that the power has expired or has been revoked by the death or bankruptcy of the donor or the death, mental incapacity or bankruptcy of the attorney or, if the attorney is a body corporate, its winding up or dissolution;

(e)   on being satisfied that the power was not a valid subsisting enduring power when registration was effected;

(f)   on being satisfied that fraud or undue pressure was used to induce the donor to create the power; or

(g)   on being satisfied that, having regard to all the cirumstances and in particular the attorney's relationship to or connection with the donor, the attorney is unsuitable to be the donor's attorney.

(5) Where the court cancels the registration of an instrument on being satisfied of the matters specified in paragraph (f) or (g) of subsection (4) above it shall by order revoke the power created by the instrument.

(6) On the cancellation of the registration of an instrument under subsection (4) above except paragraph (c) the instrument shall be delivered up to be cancelled, unless the court otherwise directs.

Protection of attorney and third parties

Protection of attorney and third persons where power invalid or revoked

9.–(1) Subsections (2) and (3) below apply where an instrument which did not create a valid power of attorney has been registered under section 6 (whether or not the registration has been cancelled at the time of the act or transaction in question).

(2) An attorney who acts in pursuance of the power shall not incur any liability (either to the donor or to any other person) by reason of the non-existence of the power unless at the time of acting he knows –

(a) that the instrument did not create a valid enduring power; or

(b) that an event has occurred which, if the instrument had created a valid enduring power, would have had the effect of revoking the power; or

(c) that, if the instrument had created a valid enduring power, the power would have expired before that time.

(3) Any transaction between the attorney and another person shall, in favour of that person, be as valid as if the power had then been in existence, unless at the time of the transaction that person has knowledge of any of the matters mentioned in subsection (2) above.

(4) Where the interest of a purchaser depends on whether a transaction between the attorney and another person was valid by virtue of subsection (3) above, it shall be conclusively presumed in favour of the purchaser that the transaction was valid if –

(a) the transaction between that person and the attorney was completed within twelve months of the date on which the instrument was registered; or

(b) that person makes a statutory declaration, before or within three months after the completion of the purchase, that he had no reason at the time of the transaction to doubt that the attorney had authority to dispose of the property which was the subject of the transaction.

(5) For the purposes of section 5 of the Powers of Attorney Act 1971 (protection of attorney and third persons where action is taken under the power of attorney in ignorance of its having been revoked) in its application to an enduring power the revocation of which by the donor is by virtue of section 7(1)(a) above invalid unless and until confirmed by the court under section 8(3) above, knowledge of the confirmation of the revocation is, but knowledge of the unconfirmed revocation is not, knowledge of the revocation of the power.

(6) Schedule 2 shall have effect to confer protection in cases where the

instrument failed to create a valid enduring power and the power has been revoked by the donor's mental capacity.

(7) In this section 'purchaser' and 'purchase' have the meanings specified in section 205(1) of the Law of Property Act 1925.

Supplementary

Application of Mental Health Act provisions relating to the court

10.–(1) The provisions of Part VII of the Mental Health Act 1983 (relating to the Court of Protection) specified below shall apply to persons within and proceedings under this Act in accordance with the following paragraphs of this subsection and subsection (2) below, that is to say –

(a)   section 103 (functions of Visitors) shall apply to persons within this Act as it applies to the persons mentioned in that section;

(b)   section 104 (powers of judge) shall apply to proceedings under this Act with respect to persons within this Act as it applies to the proceedings mentioned in subsection (1) of that section;

(c)   section 105(1) (appeals to nominated judge) shall apply to any decision of the Master of the Court of Protection or any nominated officer in proceedings under this Act as it applies to any decision to which that subsection applies and an appeal shall lie to the Court of Appeal from any decision of a nominated judge whether given in the exercise of his original jurisdiction or on the hearing of an appeal under section 105(1) as extended by this paragraph;

(d)   section 106 except subsection (4) (rules of procedure) shall apply to proceedings under this Act and persons within this Act as it applies to the proceedings and persons mentioned in that section.

(2) Any functions conferred or imposed by the provisions of the said Part VII applied by subsection (1) above shall be exercisable also for the purposes of this Act and the persons who are 'within this Act' are the donors of and attorneys under enduring powers of attorney whether or not they would be patients for the purposes of the said Part VII.

(3) In this section 'nominated judge' and 'nominated officer' have the same meanings as in Part VII of the Mental Health Act 1983.

Application to joint and joint and several attorneys

11.–(1) An instrument which appoints more than one person to be an attorney cannot create an enduring power unless the attorneys are appointed to act jointly or jointly and severally.

(2) This Act, in its application to joint attorneys, applies to them collectively as it applies to a single attorney but subject to the modifications specified in Part I of Schedule 3.

(3) This Act, in its application to joint and several attorneys, applies with the modifications specified in subsections (4) to (7) below and in Part II of Schedule 3.

(4) A failure, as respects any one attorney, to comply with the requirements for the creation of enduring powers, shall prevent the instrument from creating such a power in his case without however affecting its efficacy for that purpose as respects the other or others or its efficacy in his case for the purpose of creating a power of attorney which is not an enduring power.

(5) Where one or more but not both or all the attorneys makes or joins in making an application for registration of the instrument then –

(a) an attorney who is not an applicant as well as one who is may act pending the initial determination of the application as provided in section 1(2) (or under section 5);

(b) notice of the application shall also be given under Schedule 1 to the other attorney or attorneys; and

(c) objection may validly be taken to the registration on a ground relating to an attorney or to the power of an attorney who is not an applicant as well as to one or the power of one who is an applicant.

(6) The court shall not refuse under section 6(6) to register an instrument because a ground of objection to an attorney or power is established if an enduring power subsists as respects some attorney who is not affected thereby but shall give effect to it by the prescribed qualification of the registration.

(7) The court shall not cancel the registration of an instrument under section 8(4) for any of the causes vitiating registration specified in that subsection if an enduring power subsists as respects some attorney who is not affected thereby but shall give effect to it by the prescribed qualification of the registration.

(8) In this section –

'prescribed' means prescribed by rules of the court; and

'the requirements for the creation of enduring powers' means the provisions of section 2 other than subsection (10) to (12) and of regulations under subsection (2) of that section.

Power of Lord Chancellor to modify pre-registration requirements in certain cases

12.–(1) The Lord Chancellor may by order exempt attorneys of such descriptions as he thinks fit from the requirements of this Act to give notice to relatives prior to registration.

(2) Subject to subsection (3) below, where an order is made under this section with respect to attorneys of a specified description then, during the currency of the order, this Act shall have effect in relation to any attorney of that description with the omission of so much of section 4(3) and Schedule 1 as requires notice of an application for registration to be given to relatives.

(3) Notwithstanding that an attorney under a joint or joint and several

power is of a description specified in a current order under this section, subsection (2) above shall not apply in relation to him if any of the other attorneys under the power is not of a description specified in that or another current order under this section.

(4) The power to make an order under this section shall be exercisable by statutory instrument which shall be subject to annulment in pursuance of a resolution of either House of Parliament.

Interpretation

13.–(1) In this Act –

'the court', in relation to any functions under this Act, means the authority having jurisdiction under Part VII of the Mental Health Act 1983;

'enduring power' is to be construed in accordance with section 2;

'mentally incapable' or 'mental incapacity', except where it refers to revocation at common law, means, in relation to any person, that he is incapable by reason of mental disorder of managing and administering his property and affairs and 'mentally capable' and 'mental capacity' shall be construed accordingly;

'mental disorder' has the same meaning as it has in the Mental Health Act 1983;

'notice' means notice in writing;

'rules of the court' means rules under Part VII of the Mental Health Act 1983 as applied by section 10;

'statutory maximum' has the meaning given by section 74(1) of the Criminal Justice Act 1982;

'trust corporation' means the Public Trustee or a corporation either appointed by the High Court or a county court (according to their respective jurisdictions) in any particular case to be a trustee or entitled by rules under section 4(3) of the Public Trustee Act 1906 to act as custodian trustee.

(2) Any question arising under or for the purposes of this Act as to what the donor of the power might at any time be expected to do shall be determined by assuming that he had full mental capacity at the time but otherwise by reference to the circumstances existing at that time.

Short title, commencement and extent

14.–(1) This Act may be cited as the Enduring Powers of Attorney Act 1985.

(2) This Act shall come into force on such day as the Lord Chancellor appoints by order made by statutory instrument.

(3) This Act extends to England and Wales only except that section 7(3) and section 10(1)(b) so far as it applies section 104(4) of the Mental Health Act 1983 extend also to Scotland and Northern Ireland.

Schedules

Section 4(3)   SCHEDULE 1

NOTIFICATION PRIOR TO REGISTRATION

PART I

DUTY TO GIVE NOTICE TO RELATIVES AND DONOR

Duty to give notice to relatives

1. Subject to paragraph 3 below, before making an application for registration the attorney shall give notice of his intention to do so to all those persons (if any) who are entitled to receive notice by virtue of paragraph 2 below.

2.–(1) Subject to the limitations contained in sub-paragraphs (2) to (4) below, persons of the following classes (referred to in this Act as 'relatives') are entitled to receive notice under paragraph 1 above –

(a)   the donor's husband or wife;

(b)   the donor's children;

(c)   the donor's parents;

(d)   the donor's brothers and sisters, whether of the whole or half blood;

(e)   the widow or widower of a child of the donor;

(f)   the donor's grandchildren;

(g)   the children of the donor's brothers and sisters of the whole blood;

(h)   the children of the donor's brothers and sisters of the half blood;

(i)   the donor's uncles and aunts of the whole blood; and

(j)   the children of the donor's uncles and aunts of the whole blood.

(2) A person is not entitled to receive notice under paragraph 1 above if –

(a)   his name or address is not known to the attorney and cannot be reasonably ascertained by him; or

(b)   the attorney has reason to believe that he has not attained eighteen years or is mentally incapable.

(3) Except where sub-paragraph (4) below applies, no more than three persons are entitled to receive notice under paragraph 1 above and, in determining the persons who are so entitled, persons falling within class (a) of sub-paragraph (1) above are to be preferred to persons falling within class (b) of that sub-paragraph, persons falling within class (b) are to be preferred to persons falling within class (c) of that sub-paragraph; and so on.

(4) Notwithstanding the limit of three specified in sub-paragraph (3) above, where –

(a)   there is more than one person falling within any of classes (a) to (j) of sub-paragraph (1) above, and

(b)   at least one of those persons would be entitled to receive notice under paragraph 1 above,

then subject to sub-paragraph (2) above, all the persons falling within that class are entitled to receive notice under paragraph 1 above.

3.–(1) An attorney shall not be required to give notice under paragraph 1 above to himself or to any other attorney under the power who is joining in making the application, notwithstanding that he or, as the case may be, the other attorney is entitled to receive notice by virtue of paragraph 2 above.

(2) In the case of any person who is entitled to receive notice under paragraph 1 above, the attorney, before applying for registration, may make an application to the court to be dispensed from the requirement to give him notice; and the court shall grant the application if it is satisfied –

(a)   that it would be undesirable or impracticable for the attorney to give him notice; or

(b)   that no useful purpose is likely to be served by giving him notice.

Duty to give notice to donor

4.–(1) Subject to sub-paragraph (2) below, before making an application for registration the attorney shall give notice of his intention to do so to the donor.

(2) Paragraph 3(2) above shall apply in relation to the donor as it applies in relation to a person who is entitled to receive notice under paragraph 1 above.

PART II

CONTENTS OF NOTICES

5. Notice to relatives under this Schedule –

(a)   shall be in the prescribed form;

(b)   shall state that the attorney proposes to make an application to the Court of Protection for the registration of the instrument creating the enduring power in question;

(c)   shall inform the person to whom it is given that he may object to the proposed registration by notice in writing to the Court of Protection before the expiry of the period of four weeks beginning with the day on which the notice under this Schedule was given to him;

(d)   shall specify, as the grounds on which an objection to registration may be made, the grounds set out in section 6(5).

6. A notice to the donor under this Schedule –

(a)   shall be in the prescribed form;

(b)   shall contain the statement mentioned in paragraph 5(b) above; and

(c)   shall inform the donor that, whilst the instrument remains registered, any revocation of the power by him will be ineffective unless and until the revocation is confirmed by the Court of Protection.

PART III

DUTY TO GIVE NOTICE TO OTHER ATTORNEYS

7.–(1) Subject to sub-paragraph (2) below, before making an application for registration an attorney under a joint and several power shall give notice of his intention to do so to any other attorney under the power who is not joining in making the application; and paragraphs 3(2) and 5 above shall apply in relation to attorneys entitled to receive notice by virtue of this paragraph as they apply in relation to persons entitled to receive notice by virtue of paragraph 2 above.

(2) An attorney is not entitled to receive notice by virtue of this paragraph if –

(a)   his address is not known to the applying attorney and cannot reasonably be ascertained by him; or

(b)   the applying attorney has reason to believe that he has not attained eighteen years or is mentally incapable.

PART IV

SUPPLEMENTARY

8.–(1) For the purposes of this Schedule an illegitimate child shall be treated as if he were the legitimate child of his mother and father.

(2) Notwithstanding anything in section 7 of the Interpretation Act 1978 (construction of references to service by post), for the purposes of this Schedule a notice given by post shall be regarded as given on the date on which it was posted.

Section 9(6)   SCHEDULE 2

FURTHER PROTECTION OF ATTORNEY AND THIRD PERSON

1. Where –

(a)   an instrument framed in a form prescribed under section 2(2) creates a power which is not a valid enduring power; and

(b)   the power is revoked by the mental incapacity of the donor,

paragraphs 2 and 3 below shall apply, whether or not the instrument has been registered.

2. An attorney who acts in pursuance of the power shall not, by reason of the revocation, incur any liability (either to the donor or to any other person) unless at the time of acting he knows –

(a)   that the instrument did not create a valid and enduring power; and

(b)   that the donor has become mentally incapable.

3. Any transaction between the attorney and another person shall, in favour of that person, be as valid as if the power had then been in existence, unless at the time of the transaction that person knows –

(a)   that the instrument did not create a valid enduring power; and

(b)   that the donor has become mentally incapable

4. Section 9(4) shall apply for the purpose of determining whether a transaction was valid by virtue of paragraph 3 above as it applies for the purpose of determining whether a transaction was valid by virtue of section 9(3).

Section 11(2)(3)   **SCHEDULE 3**

JOINT AND JOINT AND SEVERAL ATTORNEYS

PART I

JOINT ATTORNEYS

1. In this section 2(7), the reference to the time when the attorney executes the instrument shall be read as a reference to the time when the second or last attorney executes the instrument.

2. In section 2(9) and (10), the reference to the attorney shall be read as a reference to any attorney under the power.

3. In section 5, references to the attorney shall be read as including references to any attorney under the power.

4. Section 6 shall have effect as if the ground of objection to the registration of the instrument specified in subsection (5)(e) applied to any attorney under the power.

5. In section 8(2), references to the attorney shall be read as including references to any attorney under the power.

6. In section 8(4), references to the attorney shall be read as including references to any attorney under the power.

PART II

JOINT AND SEVERAL ATTORNEYS

7. In section 2(10), the reference to the bankruptcy of the attorney shall be construed as a reference to the bankruptcy of the last remaining attorney under the power; and the bankruptcy of any other attorney under the power shall cause that person to cease to be attorney, whatever the circumstances of the bankruptcy.

8. The restriction upon disclaimer imposed by section 4(6) applies only to those attorneys who have reason to believe that the donor is or is becoming mentally incapable.

Appendix 3

Forms

Contents

Enduring Power of Attorney

Part A: About using this form

1. **You may choose one attorney or more than one.** If you choose one attorney then you must delete everything between the square brackets on the first page of the form. If you choose more than one, you must decide whether they are able to act:
   - Jointly (that is, they must all act together and cannot act separately) or
   - Jointly and severally (that is, they can all act together but they can also act separately if they wish).

   On the first page of the form, show what you have decided by crossing out one of the alternatives.

2. **If you give your attorney(s) general power** in relation to all your property and affairs, it means that they will be able to deal with your money or property and may be able to sell your house.

3. **If you don't want your attorney(s) to have such wide powers**, you can include any restrictions you like. For example, you can include a restriction that your attorney(s) must not act on your behalf until they have reason to believe that you are becoming mentally incapable; or a restriction as to what your attorney(s) may do. Any restrictions you choose must be written or typed where indicated on the second page of the form.

4. **If you are a trustee** (and please remember that co-ownership of a home involves trusteeship), you should seek legal advice if you want your attorney(s) to act as a trustee on your behalf.

5. **Unless you put in a restriction preventing it** your attorney(s) will be able to use any of your money or property to make any provision which you yourself might be expected to make for their own needs or the needs of other people. Your attorney(s) will also be able to use your money to make gifts, but only for reasonable amounts in relation to the value of your money and property.

6. **Your attorney(s) can recover the out-of-pocket expenses** of acting as your attorney(s). If your attorney(s) are professional people, for example solicitors or accountants, they may be able to charge for their professional services as well. You may wish to provide expressly for remuneration of your attorney(s) (although if they are trustees they may not be allowed to accept it).

7. **If your attorney(s) have reason to believe** that you have become or are becoming mentally incapable of managing your affairs, your attorney(s) will have to apply to the Court of Protection for registration of this power.

8. **Before applying to the Court of Protection for registration** of this power, your attorney(s) must give written notice that that is what they are going to do, to you and your nearest relatives as defined in the Enduring Powers of Attorney Act 1985. You or your relatives will be able to object if you or they disagree with registration.

9. **This is a simplified explanation** of what the Enduring Powers of Attorney Act 1985 and the Rules and Regulations say. If you need more guidance, you or your advisers will need to look at the Act itself and the Rules and Regulations. The Rules are the Court of Protection (Enduring Powers of Attorney) Rules 1986) (Statutory Instrument 1986 No 127). The Regulations are the Enduring Powers of Attorney (Prescribed Form) Regulations 1990 (Statutory Instrument 1990 No 1376).

10. Note to Attorney(s)
    After the power has been registered you should notify the Court of Protection if the donor dies or recovers.

11. Note to Donor
    Some of these explanatory notes may not apply to the form you are using if it has already been adapted to suit your particular requirements.

You can cancel this power at any time before it has to be registered.

Part B: To be completed by the 'donor' (the person appointing the attorney(s))

Don't sign this form unless you understand what it means

Please read the notes in the margin which follow and which are part of the form itself.

Donor's name and address.

Donor's date of birth.

See note 1 on the front of this form. If you are appointing only one attorney you should cross out everything between the square brackets. If appointing more than two attorneys please give the additional name(s) on an attached sheet.

Cross out the one which does not apply (see note 1 on the front of this form).

Cross out the one which does not apply (see note 2 on the front of this form). Add any additional powers.

If you don't want the attorney(s) to have general power, you must give details here of what authority you are giving the attorney(s).

Cross out the one which does not apply.

I _____

of _____

born on _____

appoint _____

of _____

• [and _____

of _____

• jointly
• jointly and severally]
to be my attorney(s) for the purpose of the Enduring Powers of Attorney Act 1985
   • with general authority to act on my behalf
   • with authority to do the following on my behalf:

in relation to
• all my property and affairs
• the following property and affairs:

210

Please read the notes in the margin which follow and which are part of the form itself.

If there are restrictions or conditions, insert them here; if not, cross out these words if you wish (see note 3 on the front of this form).

If this form is being signed at your direction:-
• the person signing must not be an attorney or any witness (to Parts B or C).
• you must add a statement that this form has been signed at your direction.
• a second witness is necessary (please see below).
Your signature (or mark).

Date.

Someone must witness your signature.

Signature of witness. Your attorney(s) cannot be your witness. It is not advisable for your husband or wife to be your witness.

A second witness is only necessary if this form is not being signed by you personally but at your direction (for example, if a physical disability prevents you from signing).

Signature of second witness.

• subject to the following restrictions and conditions:

I intend that this power shall continue even if I become mentally incapable

I have read or have had read to me the notes in Part A which are part of, and explain, this form.

Signed by me as a deed and delivered

on _____

in the presence of   _____

Full name of witness   _____

Address of witness   _____

_____

_____

in the presence of   _____

Full name of witness   _____

Address of witness   _____

_____

_____

SPECIMEN

Part C: To be completed by the attorney(s)

Note 1. This form may be adapted to provide for execution by a corporation

2. If there is more than one attorney additional sheets in the form as shown below must be added to this part C

Please read the notes in the margin which follow and which are part of the form itself.

Don't sign this form before the donor has signed Part B or if, in your opinion, the donor was already mentally incapable at the time of signing Part B.

If this form is being signed at your direction:-
- the person signing must not be an attorney or any witness (to Parts B or C).
- you must add a statement that this form has been signed at your direction
- a second witness is necessary (please see below).

Signature (or mark) of attorney

Date.

Signature of witness.

The attorney must sign the form and his signature must be witnessed. The donor may not be the witness and one attorney may not witness the signature of the other.

A second witness is only necessary if this form is not being signed by you personally but at your direction (for example, if a physical disability prevents you from signing).
Signature of second witness.

I understand that I have a duty to apply to the Court for the registration of this form under the Enduring Powers of Attorney Act 1985 when the donor is becoming or has become mentally incapable.

I also understand my limited power to use the donor's property to benefit persons other than the donor.

I am not a minor.

SPECIMEN

Signed by me as a deed and delivered _____

on _____

in the presence of   _____

Full name of witness   _____

Address of witness   _____

_____

_____

in the presence of   _____

Full name of witness   _____

Address of witness   _____

_____

_____

212

FORM EP1

Court of Protection/Public Trust Office
Enduring Powers of Attorney Act 1985

Notice of intention to apply for registration

To ....

of ....

This form may be adapted for use by three or more attorneys.

Give the name and address of the donor.

It will be necessary for you to produce evidence in support of your objection. If evidence is available please send it with your objection, the attorney(s) will be given an opportunity to respond to your objection.

The grounds upon which you can object are limited and are shown at 2 overleaf.

TAKE NOTICE THAT

I ....

of ....

and I ....

of ....

the attorney(s) of ....

....

of ....

....

intend apply to the Public Trustee for registration of the enduring power of attorney appointing me (us) attorney(s) and made by the donor on the

....19 ....

1. If you wish to object to the proposed registration you have 4 weeks from the day on which this notice is given to you to do so in writing. Any objections should be sent to the Public Trustee and should contain the following details:

- your name and address;
- any relationship to the donor;
- if you are not the donor, the name and address of the donor;
- the name and address of the attorney;
- the grounds for objecting to the registration of the enduring power.

Note. The instrument means the enduring power of attorney made by the donor which it is sought to register.

The attorney(s) does not have to be a relative. Relatives are not entitled to know of the existnece of the enduring power of attorney prior to being given this notice.

2. The grounds on which you may object are:

- that the power purported to have been created by the instrument is not valid as an enduring power of attorney;

- that the power created by the instrument no longer subsists;

- that the application is premature because the donor is not yet becoming mentally incapable;

- that fraud or undue pressure was used to induce the donor to make the power;

- that the attorney is unsuitable to be the donor's attorney (having regard to all the circumstances and in particular the attorney's relationship to or connection with the donor).

Note. This is addressed only to the donor.

3. You are informed that while the enduring power of attorney remains registered, you will not be able to revoke it until the Court of Protection confirms the revocation.

Note. This notice should be signed by every one of the attorneys who are applying to register the enduring power of attorney.

Signed ....Dated ....

Signed ....Dated ....

FORM EP2

Court of Protection/Public Trust Office
Enduring Powers of Attorney Act 1985

No. ....

Application for registration

Note. Give the full name and present address of the donor. If the donor's address on the enduring power of attorney is different give that one too.

The donor

Name ....
Address ....
....
Address on the Enduring Power of Attorney (if different) ....
....

Note. Give the full name(s) and details of the attorney(s)

The attorney(s)

Name ....
Address ....
age .... occupation ....
relationship to donor (if any) ....

Name ....
Address ....
age .... occupation ....
relationship to donor (if any) ....

This form may be adapted for use by three or more attorneys

The date is the date upon which the donor signed the enduring power of attorney

I (we) the attorney(s) apply to register the enduring power of attorney made by the donor under the above Act on

the.. 19 ....
the original of which accompanies this application

I (we) have reason to believe that the donor is or is becoming mentally incapable

---

Notice must be personally given. It should be made clear if someone other than the attorney(s) gives the notice

I (we) have given notice in the prescribed form to the following:

• the donor personally at ....
....
on the.. 19 ....

SPECIMEN

If there are no relatives entitled to notice please say so

● The following relatives of the donor at the addresses below on the dates given:

Names	Relationship	addresses	date

Note. Cross out this section if it does not apply.

● The Co-Attorney(s)...

    at...

    on...

A remittance for the registration fee accompanies this application

Note. The application should be signed by all the attorneys who are making the application.

I(we) certify that the above information is correct and that to the best of my(our) knowledge and belief I(we) have complied with the provisions of the Enduring Powers of Attorney Act 1985 and of all the Rules and Regulations under it.

Signed .... Dated.......................

Signed .... Dated.......................

....

This must not pre-date the date(s) when the notices were given

Address to which correspondence relating to the application is to be sent if different to that of the first-named attorney making this application

....

....

FORM EP3

Court of Protection/Public Trust Office
Enduring Powers of Attorney Act 1985
In the matter of a power given by

If this application is being made prior to an application for registration the original enduring power of attorney should accompany this application

....(a donor)

to ....(attorney)

and ....(attorney)

General form of application

I..

of ....

and I..

of ....

Apply for an order or directions that ....

....

....

....

....

....

....

and for any other directions which are necessary as a result of my/our application.

The grounds on which I/we make this application are:

....

....

....

....

Note. Give details of the order or directions that you are seeking

State under which sub-section of the Enduring Powers of Attorney Act 1985 or which rule of the Court of Protection (Enduring Powers of Attorney) Rules 1994 this application is made

Note. Give details of the grounds on which you are seeking the order or directions

Evidence in support should accompany this application

Note. This application should be signed by all the applicants or their solicitors

Signed .... Dated.......................

Signed .... Dated.......................

Address where notices should be sent ....

....

....

Index